Modern Democracies:
Economic Power
versus
Political Power

Modern Democracies: Economic Power versus Political Power

Maurice Duverger

University of Paris, The Sorbonne
Translated by Charles L. Markmann

The Dryden Press
901 North Elm Street
Hinsdale, Illinois 60521

Note on the translation:

The translator wishes to thank Frances Thompson for the invaluable help she gave him in translating this volume.

After the translation had been completed, the author rewrote a number of sections and this new material was translated by Mrs. Jacklyn Macridis.

Contents

Contents

Contents

Modern Democracies:
Economic Power
versus
Political Power

Introduction

The United States, Canada, Western Europe (with the exceptions of Greece, Spain, and Portugal), Australia, and New Zealand possess equivalent political institutions, similar economic structures, approximately equal levels of development, roughly the same moral and religious beliefs, and congruent cultural traditions. Of course, there are marked differences between American presidentialism and European parliamentarianism, between the Scandinavian and the Italian governments, between French and American capitalism, between Swedish and Italian average incomes, between the Catholic church and the Protestant denominations, between northern and Latin moral codes, between the cultures of Paris and New York. But these differences are secondary in relation to the basic common traits that give the whole an easily recognizable physiognomy. What is called the Western system is the amalgam formed by the linking together of these political institutions, economic structures, levels of development, religious and moral beliefs, and cultural traditions. The Western system has been adopted also by Israel, Turkey, Lebanon, Japan, India, Ceylon, and a few other nations; but in each of these countries it has been combined with specific elements that have modified its structure in varying degrees.

The Western system is characterized by the existence of competitive elections, in which a number of candidates take part and the voters can choose among them with considerable freedom. Not all the candidates have equal campaign facilities, because of differences in financial resources or government backing. Nevertheless, each candidate can make himself heard, and each voter can make his selection without being subjected to excessive external pressures. The victors are subject to a periodic reappraisal by the electors (usually every four to seven years) that can lead to their removal from power. Therefore, they are

1

obliged to take into account the views of the governed to a far greater extent than do rulers in those systems in which power is lifelong, without any challenge from the citizenry.

Competition ranges over the whole life of society. Opinions, beliefs, ideologies can vie with one another through the various means of expression and information: press, books, theater, movies, radio, television, and so on. Freedom is never complete. There are always censorships, public or private, and the range of confrontation is sometimes quite narrow: socialism has little place in the United States; communism has few adherents except in France, Italy, Finland, Luxembourg, and Iceland. Moreover, social conditioning by the mass media is becoming increasingly stronger. But the confrontation remains real nonetheless, in sharp contrast to the monolithic systems of the various dictatorships.

Elections and pluralism place a limitation on the rulers that constitutes another essential element in the Western system. In the 1930s, the word *totalitarian* was applied to modern autocratic systems to make clear that their rulers claimed to govern the whole of human activities (including art, thought, religion, love, leisure, and play) and admitted no distinction between public and private life. In contrast, the Western system is "limited"; in it the rulers control only certain areas of human activity, leaving the citizens to do as they please in the others. Unquestionably, the public sector tends to grow larger and larger in technologically advanced states. Nevertheless, large areas of activity remain beyond the reach of government. Various institutions assure this limitation on the rulers, not only periodic elections and pluralism but also the separation between the executive and the legislature, the existence of independent tribunals, the principle of the rule of law, the restrictions of constitutions, decentralization, and so forth.

Underlying these institutions are an ideology and a system of values that justify and sustain them: liberalism. It can be summarized in the words of Article I of the Declaration of the Rights of Man and the Citizen, promulgated by the French in 1789: "All men are born and remain free and equal in their rights." This means, first of all, that no one can benefit by inherited privileges that elevate him above his fellow citizens, and that every man can think, express himself, and behave as he sees fit, the freedom of others being the only curb on the freedom of each. The freedom of the physical person through the right of *habeas corpus*; the sanctity of the home; the inviolability of correspondence; the right to move about at will; freedom to marry by mutual choice and consent and to divorce on the same basis; the right to raise one's children according to one's beliefs; freedom of thought and of its expression, of assembly, of protest, of association; economic freedoms founded on private property, free enterprise, and freedom to work and to travel—all these constitute a coherent whole that tends to subordinate the community to the individual or, more precisely, to make the community an association of individuals each of whom acts according to his own impulses, which he regulates through self-discipline. An optimistic philosophy of trust in the natural goodness of man is at the core of this liberal ideology.

The economic and social aspects of the Western system cannot be divorced from its political and ideological traits. Its economic freedoms constitute what is called free enterprise by liberals and capitalism by Socialists. The means of production (land, tools, factories, warehouses, offices) are objects of acquisition by certain men, while others have only their ability to work, which they hire out to the owners. The inequality between the two classes, which was considerable in the nineteenth century, has been diminished today through the efforts of the great labor organizations. Socialists emphasize the darker side of capitalism exemplified by this inequality; whereas its champions insist on its brighter side: its capacity for innovation and change, its efficiency, its productivity. Is it not the liberal nations that have attained the highest stage of economic development?

The causal relation between the two phenomena is open to argument. Western Europe's technological superiority over Eastern Europe, for instance, may derive from initial geographical advantages and favorable historical development, rather than from any superiority of capitalism over socialism, which is yet to be demonstrated. In any event, liberalism exists, by and large, in the rich nations. Some think that these two elements—liberalism and advanced economic development—are interdependent. Free elections, pluralism, and civil liberties can develop only if class conflicts and social tensions in general decline and if the population as a whole enjoys a level of education that makes possible the real exercise of the rights of the citizen. These elements, obviously, presuppose a high level of economic development.

Another feature of the Western system ought not to be overlooked.

Although the Western system is rationalist, it functions in countries which espouse the Christian religion. In the Catholic countries there have been conflicts between liberal ideology and the church, at any rate until the Second Vatican Council; in these countries liberal ideology has taken over the essential elements of Christian morality and secularized them. In the Protestant countries, ideology has generally developed in harmony with religion. In some Lutheran countries and in Great Britain, the Western rulers have remained officially religious leaders, too, and this can lead to strange situations. Less than twenty years ago the Norwegian Parliament was almost compelled to decide by law whether hell existed. In the United States, the government is entirely secular, but religion plays a very large part in ideology and in daily life.

Finally, the Western system is founded on the humanist culture that originated in ancient Greek civilization. This civilization was expanded and popularized by the Romans, who carried it throughout the Mediterranean area and into western Europe. It interbred with indigenous elements, in varying degrees, according to regions. Scandinavia, Germany, and the British Isles were less influenced than were Italy, France, and Spain by this Greek and Roman culture. A northern culture and a southern culture have more or less confronted each other throughout history. The traces of this confrontation persist in our own day; they affect political attitudes and social behavior patterns. The Renaissance revived ancient art and thought, and since then the Greek and Latin languages and the classical authors have formed the basis of the education of the Western European ruling classes. The United States, built by European emigrants, has the same cultural foundations. But that country's autonomous growth over the past two centuries has made it more pragmatic and suspicious of abstract ideas, thus separating it rather profoundly from the classical traditions still generally adhered to in Europe.

So, like Janus, the two-faced god whose portrait was stamped on the coins of the Roman republic twenty-two centuries ago, the Western system offers opposing yet complementary aspects, and this dualism constitutes its essential nature. On the one hand, pluralism, freedoms, and competitive elections offer its citizens greater possibilities of influencing their governors than are to be found anywhere else. While these rights were for a long time more apparent than real, and to a certain extent may still be so, in the past fifty years they have acquired a degree of reality that cannot be seriously disputed. It is no longer a matter of "formal" democracy, as it was in the nineteenth century, when Marx was elaborating his analysis; it is now genuine democracy.

On the other hand, this democracy is less than total. In the Western countries, the citizens and their organizations are not the sole possessors of political power. They share it chiefly with the owners of capital, both the individuals and, especially, the great industrial, commercial, and financial firms. This is Janus' other face. Legislators, ministers, and chiefs of government are not mere puppets in the hands of capitalists, as simplistic propaganda would have it. They can seek support from the voters when they resist the pressure of the economic potentates; but that pressure is strong, the more so because it can also exert great influence on the electorate. Political decisions are made within an arena in which the two principal forces are the voters and the rich capitalists. Because political power in these countries is based both on the people (*demos*) and on wealth (*plutos*), we call the political system "plutodemocracy."

This term *plutodemocracy* has the advantage not only of being accurate but also of being neutral, balancing as it does a positive and a negative characterization. One of the difficulties of political science is the use of terms that are not objective. The terms almost always imply a value judgment. To contrast the liberal nations with the dictatorships is not merely to define two concrete types of political systems but also to set up a "good" against a "bad" system, the liberal being the good and the dictatorship the bad in almost all contemporary value scales. Along the same lines, *plutocracy* means a bad system and *democracy* a good one; by combining the two, one achieves a certain objectivity of vocabulary.

The relative novelty of the term should not mask the triteness of the fact. Neither of the elements of plutodemocracy, as I have identified them, is original. No more is their juxtaposition. The links between, on the one hand, pluralist elections, parliaments, and public liberties and, on the other hand, capitalism and the market economy—like those between liberal ideologies, the Christian religion, and the cultural traditions of humanism—have long since been recognized and analyzed. Other students, frequently in excellent works, have already undertaken to synthesize the essential characteristics of modern Western institutions. My endeavor, however, is profoundly different from theirs; mine

5

consists in taking up the elements that have just been described as constituting a "system," regarding them in the precise sense of the term, and studying them as such.

What this means is that these elements are treated as a coherent, structured whole, of which all the parts are interdependent, and which reacts integrally to changes in its environment, as would a living organism or a cybernetic machine, whether it adapts itself through a kind of self-adjustment, undergoes resulting modification, or succeeds in undoing the external changes. The purpose of this book is to analyze plutodemocracy as a system. Despite appearances, such an undertaking is quite different from studies in "comparative government." Instead of comparing existing systems, taken as basic entities, to clarify their likenesses and differences, I am taking the Western system as the basic entity, in which each country represents an adaptation to specific conditions. From this point of view, only the origin of the system and its development under external pressures make it possible to grasp its essential mechanisms and the significance of its current changes.

The concept of a system as it is used in this book is no more original than the rest. It virtually conforms to Talcott Parsons' well-known statement: "When a group of interdependent phenomena gives evidence of a sufficiently definite arrangement and of stability in time, one can say that it possesses a structure and that it would be profitable to treat it as a system."[1] It is even closer to the notion of "structure" developed by Jean Piaget. I prefer the former term because it is more open to genetic and evolutionary analysis. It should be noted that what I designate the "system" remains closer to facts, less formalized and less abstract, than the theoretical models employed today by so-called systems analysis.

It incorporates, however, only certain elements of reality, chosen because they are regarded as fundamental. A system thus constructed constitutes only a hypothesis and nothing more. Interpretation of Western institutions in this form is no more "valid" than interpretation based on individual systems, functionalist interpretations, or any others. It is to be hoped only that it is more "operational"—that is, that it more effectively makes possible the understanding of pluto-

1. T. Parsons, E. Shils, K. D. Naegde, and J. T. Pitts, *Theories of Society* (Glencoe, Ill.: Free Press, 1961), Vol. I, p. 21.

democracy. If such be the case, it means that in a certain fashion it corresponds to the facts. But there is always the question of the interpretation of those facts.

The dog's ear, which perceives sounds inaudible to man, does not form the same overall image of auditive facts that is made by the human ear, which does not perceive some. Similarly, the faceted eye of the insect does not see the world as does the globular human eye. Synthesizing minds do not apprehend social wholes in the same way as analyzing minds: each, according to the concepts used, chooses the elements that it retains, as does the ear or the eye.

The development of a political system, as I defined it, is to a great extent shaped by the evolution of economic and technological conditions. This point, elaborated first by the Marxists, is not seriously contested today. In fact, for some decades there has been a curious convergence of Western and Marxist thought. In the United States and Western Europe, there is virtually no further challenge of the determining influence exercised by technological advances on social evolution. Today, it is too evident to be denied, and this present experience is naturally projected onto the past. The Western expression *technical progress* is almost a literal translation of the Marxist concept of *state of the forces of production*, which, for Socialists, governs systems of production, relations between classes, and all social superstructures, including political regimes, ideology, culture, and so on. But it is not simple to establish a close and direct relationship between the development of the techniques of production and the evolution of political systems. Institutions, norms, and beliefs cannot be established and cannot maintain themselves if they are in direct conflict with the forces of production. Every serious and lasting change in the conditions of production will bring about the development of new beliefs, norms, and institutions or the radical transformation of the existing ones. The basic elements that constitute a political system do not always appear in the same order. It is not necessary that the economic factors appear first. For instance, the appearance of communist regimes in Europe was due to political factors: the military defeat that brought about the collapse of czarist Russia, the Soviet victory in the Russian Revolution, and the international agreements that put Eastern Europe under the control of the Soviet Union in 1945. Communism thus appeared first in the form of a state apparatus, which in turn created the economic and collectivist structures.

This general observation, however, does not negate the primacy of economic factors. If the socialist system had not corresponded to the existing economic and technological conditions, the political and military events of 1917 and 1945 could not have accounted for its implantation in Russia and Eastern Europe, and the efforts of Stalin and Lenin would have appeared retrospectively just as utopian as the efforts of Spartacus, Savonarola, Thomas Muntzer, and so many others. The fact that the political factor precedes the economic one is of secondary importance. What counts is that the system corresponds by and large to a certain state of technology and to certain conditions of production. It is in this sense—that is, by linking the economic and the political conceptually rather than historically—that my notion of a system has operational value.

The Western political systems developed in a manner much more in conformity with the traditional Marxist scheme. The evolution of the means of production accounted for the erosion of the feudal economy and the emergence of a capitalistic one—over a period of centuries. Thus aristocracy gradually gave place to the bourgeoisie. The interests and needs of this new dominant class were expressed in terms of a new ideology, liberalism, which replaced the traditional monarchist one. The emergence of democratic institutions corresponded to the full realization of the system. It should be noted, however, that many of its essential parts appeared chronologically in the inverse order from which they manifested themselves in Communist societies.

Fundamentally, then, both democratic and Communist systems correspond to the forces of production. New industrial techniques generate capitalism, which becomes the first element of the Western system. It generates in turn its other elements: liberal ideology, parliamentary institutions, political pluralism, and so on. But capitalism is also responsible for the development of Communist ideology, which becomes the first element of the system, generating in turn the Bolshevik party, which exploits the military and political events of 1917 to establish a Communist regime, which imposes in turn a collectivist economy. It is this first Communist system which in turn inspires and imposes the "popular democracies" of Eastern Europe by exploiting the military and political events of 1945.

It must be pointed out that the order in which the various elements of the system appear has an impact upon its specific manifestations. The contrast between the liberal character of the political regimes of the West and the authoritarian character of the Communist political regimes can be explained in part by the differences in their formation. The first developed in accord with already existing economic structures that favored its appearance. It was supported by the ruling class, whose interest and aspirations it expressed. In sharp contrast, Communist regimes emerged within capitalist structures radically opposed to Communist ideology. These structures had to be completely destroyed in order for a collectivist economy to be established. The ruling classes were radically opposed to such an economy and resisted desperately.

Only a rigorous dictatorship permitted communism to be constructed under such conditions. It created institutions, patterns of behavior, and ideologies that had to be imposed by force. They crystallized into patterns of control and repression that were difficult to abandon later, despite the Marxist theory of the "withering away of the state." In contrast, the Western system was able to develop in the context of liberal political practices—only relatively so however, for violence was never totally absent in the plutodemocracies. But it was less pervasive and less repressive because it was less necessary. Other factors reinforced this trend as the Western system developed.

Part One:
The Formation of the Western System

*The Western system took shape within the interstices of a
completely different system, which one could call
"aristo-monarchical." It was based upon the juridical inequality
of men and their distribution in organized communities, each
endowed with different rights and duties. The basis for the system
was the fundamental distinction—founded on birth—between the nobles,
or aristocrats, and the non-nobles, or "villeins," the former
having a privileged status in relation to the latter. Within the
nobility itself, as with the non-nobles, there were great
inequalities of rank, which were also based upon birth. However,
a certain social mobility existed: one could climb socially
within each category and even pass from one category to another
by ennoblement.*

*Religion constituted one of the essential foundations of the
aristo-monarchical system. It was held that the inequality of
men on earth is in accordance with divine will, but that this
inequality is secondary with regard to men's equality before
God, who will banish all inequities in the life to come, which
is the true life, terrestrial existence being only an exile: a
clever means of making inequality acceptable to its victims. By
taking holy orders, the sons of the bourgeoisie or the peasantry
could—in spite of everything—attain a high station in life with
its attendant great power. The nobles, however, tended to obtain
the positions in the higher clergy: in France, all the bishops
and all the abbots in the monasteries were of aristocratic birth
in 1789. In other respects, the Church had an authoritarian
structure like the State, except for some Protestant sects that
were in fact instrumental in promoting the development
of plutodemocracy.*

*At the top of the aristocratic pyramid was the king,
first of the nobles. The monarch was considered to be a sort
of superman with a sacred character. In certain countries,
supernatural powers were attributed to him (the thaumaturgist
kings); everywhere, a crime committed against the king (lese
majesty) was a sort of sacrilege. In general, the monarch received*

a religious investiture, an "eighth sacrament," which placed him above other men. One finds here certain traits of the king-gods of oriental antiquity, transposed afterward in Rome in the cult of the emperor. Otherwise, the powers of the kings varied according to the country: very weak in Poland, they became very strong in France from the seventeenth century on, while they declined in Great Britain. The aristo-monarchical society was constantly torn by an internal contradiction between its aristocratic aspect, leaning toward the power of the nobles, and its monarchical aspect, leaning toward the power of the king. The Western system utilized this contradiction in its development, forming an alliance sometimes with the lords against the king and sometimes with the king against the lords, depending upon the situation.

Chapter One

The British Parliament: Trojan Horse of Plutodemocracy

Within the "aristo-monarchy" we find a number of discordant elements that resemble the modern Western system. Thus the reform of the religious orders in the Middle Ages had established in the monasteries the principle of elections: it gave birth to modern democratic procedures. This revived the ancient traditions of the church whereby bishops were elected by the faithful. Also in the feudal period there were representative assemblies—the king convening periodically his principal vassals in the "Grand Councils," the "King's Courts," the "Champs de mars" or the "Champs de mai," in order to ask for advice and aide—that is, personal services or gifts of money.

These institutions were full of ambiguities and contradictions. If to some extent they presaged the parliamentary elections that came later, they were at the time shot through with archaic forms: the "councils" and the "assemblies of the vassals" contained many elements that preceded the advent of the aristo-monarchy. But everything changed when the overall evolution of society brought about the coming of plutodemocracy. Then many of the antique forms were used to construct the new system, within which they were of course destined to play different roles.

The first great change in society occurred more than nine centuries ago, when various discoveries and new techniques in Western Europe led to increased agricultural production and improved means of transportation. The standard of living rose, the population grew, roads and bridges multiplied, and human contacts increased owing to religious pilgrimages and the Crusades. Instead of agricultural production primarily confined to "the farm"—or rather the feudal domain—there developed a tendency to produce with an eye to exchange and trade. Farming remained the predominant occupation, but merchants, artisans, and money-lenders began to play an increasing role in the economy. Thus a new class was formed, living in "towns": the bourgeoisie—living in the "bourgs."

The Two Historical Paths of the Bourgeoisie

The bourgeoisie is defined not only in terms of the economic activities of its members (artisans, manufacturers, merchants, tradesmen, bankers, and so on) but also in terms of its methods. With the bourgeoisie profit was the essential driving force of the economy, whereas the feudal economy was based on the exploitation of the land in terms of the traditional notions of service, community, personal fealty, privilege, rank, and status. These changes in the forces of production brought about an upheaval in the structure of values that culminated in the introduction of the Western system. But at first the new economic forces occupied a limited place when compared to the traditional forms of farming, which had maintained themselves for a long time. In the beginning the bourgeoisie was a minority and did not yet have the means to replace the aristocratic-monarchical system. It could only modify it. It succeeded at first only at the local level, by acquiring municipal freedoms through the development of "communes"—that is, autonomous towns that were independent of the jurisdiction of the nobles and the bishops or that shared power with the latter. The commune was administered by a body of elected magistrates. Its inhabitants were not subject to the forced labor and the rents of the feudal system. In order to defend themselves against possible invaders they formed militias and constructed protective ramparts around the town: therefore they no longer needed the protection of the nobility. They had their own tribunals for settling disputes and their own tax system for maintaining the town's public services. Thus the communes were like plutodemocratic islands (suffrage was limited and the rich dominated) in the sea of an aristocratic world. But their status was uncertain, for they were also collective seigniories incorporated into the feudal system: their right to have coats of arms signified their position in the feudal hierarchy.

In the fourteenth century the representation of the bourgeoisie, or the middle class, was extended beyond the municipal level to the national level, with the development of the "assemblies of estates"

14

throughout Europe. This was a matter not so much of the establishment of a new institution as of the transformation of the old feudal
ones—of the grand councils, royal courts, and so on. The innovation
consisted in the addition of a new element: the urban middle class. The
assemblies thus constituted bore various names, according to their
countries: Estates General, Cortes, Diet, Parliament, and so on. Usually
they were made up of three "estates": the clergy, the nobility, and the
middle class. In Scandinavia, however, they were composed of four
"estates": the free peasants formed a category in addition to the other
three. Each estate was represented separately: elections were held by
estates, whose representatives formed separate assemblies. As a rule, the
various assemblies did not sit together. Like the municipalities, the
assembly of each estate was ambiguous in character, perpetuating older
forms while also establishing firmly some new ones. The middle class,
for instance, elected delegates by rather modern procedures; but at the
same time, the addition of representatives from these "collective seigniories"—the communes—strengthened the feudal system. For instance,
the French assemblies of estates attempted—but failed—to set up an
elective monarchy, which would have led to an aristocratic system like
that of Poland.

Financial necessities seem to have played a preponderant part in this
transformation of feudal assemblies into the assemblies of estates. The
medieval monarch lived in a world with a closed economy, and he drew
from his own domains most of the resources required by the needs of
the state: he could therefore do without the *aide* of his vassals without
too much hardship. The monarch of the fourteenth century lived in a
very different world, in which economic trade had already developed,
more complex military techniques made armies and wars much more
expensive, and the growth of public administration called for large
resources. For such a monarch feudal *aides* had to be transformed into
modern taxes, levied against all those who had the means to pay,
notably the bourgeoisie, which was prosperous.

Brought together for the most part in order to provide funds, the
assemblies began to demand reports on the state of finances so that
they could decide whether the crown's requests were justified, to supervise the collection of taxes (in France the Estates General of 1355
organized this collection by creating a hierarchy of "the elect," who
were placed in charge of it), to insist on full details of the use of the

credits that they granted, and, finally, to audit the accounts. All this opened the way to the budgetary and fiscal powers of modern parliaments.

The assemblies of estates aspired also to political control. They lodged complaints before they granted subsidies. In England the king had to sacrifice some of his ministers in 1340 and again in 1371 in order to obtain the funds that he sought; in 1376 Parliament compelled him to have extortioners judged by the Lords. In France the Estates General of 1357 prescribed a council of guardians for the dauphin. Sometimes the kings encouraged the assemblies to take important political decisions that were favorable to the crown. The Dauphin Charles prevailed on the French Estates General of 1359 to vote down the Treaty of London made by his father. In 1399 the English Parliament approved the deposition of Richard II and the usurpation of Henry IV. In 1461 it took the side of Edward IV in the Wars of the Roses.

Two paths, then, were open to the bourgeoisie in its efforts to make a place for itself within the existing system. It could ally itself with the aristocracy by using the assemblies of estates and transforming them into true parliaments with the powers to control and limit the prerogatives of the monarch. Or, on the contrary, it could help the king rid himself of aristocratic tutelage and thus help establish an absolute monarchy. Very generally speaking, the first is the path that was followed in Great Britain and the second the one followed in continental Europe.

In specific terms the picture is obviously not so simple. The English kings at first sought alliances with the bourgeoisie just as most kings did in continental Europe, and occasionally they succeeded. On both sides of the English Channel, for instance, the movement favoring municipal rights received royal support. The opponents of such a movement were the nobles, both lay and ecclesiastic, who stood to lose their territorial jurisdiction and their revenues. In contrast, the crown had every interest in forwarding this movement in order to weaken the feudal lords and create new sources of subsidies. At the same time all the kings showed a marked preference for appointing to high administrative posts persons that came from ranks other than the nobility. Replacing the nobility, this new group of administrators became a class of civil servants characterized by competence and devotion.

16

Little by little, however, different evolutions in the alliances of nobility and bourgeoisie or king and bourgeoisie are to be noted in England and on the continent. It is the behavior of the aristocracy rather than of the bourgeoisie that becomes the principal criterion. In England an important segment of the nobility adopted capitalistic methods in the cultivation of its land and thus brought itself closer to the bourgeoisie; capitalism thus constitutes the basis of their alliance. In France, the aristocracy remained more attached to feudal practices; this set them apart from the bourgeoisie and pushed them toward an alliance with the king. In Prussia, the creation of a strong army reinforced the power of the monarch and rendered the growth of a parliamentary system difficult.

The divergences become quite clear in the seventeenth century. At the very moment when the British Parliament was engaged in a decisive conflict with the king which would lead to his execution and the temporary establishment of a republic and finally to the restoration of a weakened monarch, the assemblies on the continent began to disappear. In France the Estates General met for the last time in 1614, not to be convened again until 1789, and then in a vastly different context. In Spain, the importance of the Cortes declined after the beginning of the sixteenth century and by the end of the seventeenth century they were no longer convened in Castile. The assemblies disappeared in almost all the continental nations. Only the small nations, such as the Low Countries and the Italian republics, maintained their assemblies. In the other countries, they survived only at the local and regional level, as was the case with the provincial estates in France, and there they played a somewhat changed role: they became strongholds of the aristocracy, especially in the new territories attached to the crown. Even at the municipal level the assemblies gradually declined. In the meantime the absolute power of the monarch was steadily increasing.

Even when linked to the king, however, the continental bourgeoisie sought closer ties with the aristocracy in order to gain from its prestige. In France the middle class dreamed of titles of nobility. Molière has immortalized this desire in his *Bourgeois gentilhomme*—the bourgeois gentleman. Marrying a member of the nobility was one way for a bourgeois to acquire aristocratic status. In addition formal and public means were used, such as the granting by the king of titles of nobility to important members of the bourgeoisie in order to compensate them

17

for their services. It was subsequently established that certain offices, notably in the judiciary and the administration, would automatically ennoble their holders. In certain countries the crown began to sell offices and to increase their number in order to raise money. Thus there came into being a "nobility of the robe" (the robe was the official costume of the magistrates) that coexisted with the traditional "nobility of the sword." Like all newcomers, the ennobled burghers were often the most intransigent and the most undiscriminating supporters of the privileges of the class to which they had aspired.

Another form of incorporation into the aristocratic order was the development of the guilds of artisans and merchants. This social class was still vacillating between two courses: that of free enterprise and competition and that of defense of the social status already gained. Feudal society naturally led to the second. The urban middle class, for the greater part, allowed itself to drift into this course. It sought and received the support of the lords and the king, who gave their authorization (or "privilege") to the artisans and merchants to carry on their occupations. Thus little by little there was established a hierarchical, fixed capitalism in which only the "masters" grouped in corporations or guilds had the right to engage in a trade, assisted by their paid "journeymen" and "apprentices," whose relations with their masters were not exclusively economic, but rather paternalistic and feudal. With their banners and their armorial bearings, the guilds also gave the appearance of "collective seigniories". Thus urban society tended toward a structure analogous to that of feudal society.

In France the widespread ennoblement of members of the upper middle class brought about a veritable reversal of alliances after the reign of Louis XIV. The nobility of the robe—that is, the ennobled upper middle class—became the staunchest defender of the existing order: it assumed the responsibility of restoring the former privileges of the aristocracy. It made use of the similarity of names between the high tribunals—"parliaments"—of Paris and of the provinces that were their fiefs and the British Parliament, in order to dress its claims in modern clothing. In fact the question was still that of bringing the king under the control of the noblemen and of assuring their preeminence in the state.

But it was too late. The administrative and military machine that the middle class had helped to put into the king's hands enabled him to

18

resist the new alliance of the aristocracy and the upper middle class. And, too, this alliance was based on outmoded objectives: it aimed at the restoration of archaic institutions rather than at the creation of new ones corresponding to social evolution, as had been the case in Britain, where the union of the urban middle class and the rural gentry introduced capitalist methods to farming. In the eighteenth century the Parisian middle class adopted aristocratic methods and ideology, which no longer were adapted to the situation; the London aristocracy, on the other hand, had long since adopted middle-class methods and ideology, which corresponded to the contemporary social situation.

The Development of Parliament in Great Britain

Very quickly the British Parliament took a form different from the representative assemblies on the continent. In these assemblies each of the estates sat separately: the clergy, the nobility, the bourgeoisie, and, eventually, the peasantry. The distinction between the two chambers at Westminster was not established on the same basis. The House of Commons included not only the bourgeoisie but also members of the lower and middle nobility—the squires. The House of Lords included the members of the aristocracy and the high clergy. Each chamber represented a social class in the modern sense of the term rather than an "order" or an "estate" in the medieval sense. That the aristocracy itself was thus divided was a crucial factor in a society already dominated by the division between the nobles and the non-nobles. In order for an institution so contrary to the existing ideology and system of values to become established a number of conditions had to be met.

As previously mentioned, the impetus appears to have come from the fact that in Britain part of the landed aristocracy engaged in a capitalistic type of production based on profit. The landed aristocracy therefore became the natural ally of the middle class, which had the same economic foundation. In this way there was formed a sort of intermediate class whose productive power grew until it became dominant. The ascendancy of Parliament—the expression of this intermediate class—matched its development. In societies that were essentially agricultural, the urban middle class, restricted to its own ranks, was too weak to produce any essential changes in structure or to bring about the inception of a new political system. In these societies representative institutions, the emergence of which had been the work of the urban middle class alone, were doomed to disappear or to vegetate in a few regions. In order for them to survive and to spread, they had to find wider support, and this was what happened in Britain.

In this sense it might be said that the sheep was the sire of modern democracy. As early as the eleventh century, when England had a population of only three million, more than eight million fleeces were exported from England every year, most of them to Flanders. The county nobility that devoted itself to stock farming discovered that it had a natural community of interest with the tradesmen and wholesale merchants of the middle class. What is more, this county nobility tended to adopt the same system of values. More and more it ceased to regard land as a foundation for political and social obligations, functions, and privileges; it came to look upon land as an investment and as a source of income. The British nobleman desired to become like the bourgeois at the very time when the French bourgeoisie was aping the aristocracy. The feudal concept of service gave way to the capitalist concept of profit. To be sure, this evolution was slow, and medieval ideas persisted for a long time. R. H. Tawney regards the fifteenth century as a period of transition, in which land retained its military, political, and social importance in conjunction with its economic value.[1] The reign of the Tudors accelerated the latter tendency, which triumphed after the Civil War in the middle of the seventeenth century.

The relationship between sheep and democracy does not, however, hold everywhere. During the same period, the growth of sheep-breeding and the wool trade promoted the advent of absolute monarchy in Spain. As a matter of fact, the king relied on the owners of nomadic flocks in his struggles against the local barons. Nor did the fact that nobles practiced capitalist exploitation of their land always bring them closer to the burghers or the middle class, as it did in England. The example of the German Junker shows the possibility of other courses of development. The Junkers evolved an agriculture of the modern type within the framework of large estates worked by serfs, which was consistent with the structures of Eastern rather than of Western Europe. They imposed on the middle class their own cultural model of a paternalistic, authoritarian, and hierarchic system. Their behavior has

1. See *Religion and the Rise of Capitalism* (New York: Harcourt, Brace, 1926).

been compared with that of the Japanese aristocracy. But the Japanese nobles came into the capitalist system much later, in the nineteenth century, and participated more directly in industry. They appear to have contributed to the concentration of enterprises, thus accelerating the modernization of the country. Large contemporary firms resemble feudal seigniories in certain ways. In Japan the transition was more or less from one to the other, and one finds in present-day trusts—Mitsui, Mitsubishi, and so on—certain aspects of the behavior of the samurai of feudal Japan, although the comparison must not be exaggerated. There are many ways for the nobility to enter modern times.

The new British middle class, consisting of the squires and the bourgeoisies, was an oligarchy of a new kind. In order to find new pastures the nobility proceeded to "enclose" the common lands, that is to say, to appropriate for itself the lands previously available to all the inhabitants for common use. Later on the yeomen, that is, the peasant middle class, would do the same and appropriate for themselves lands for pasture and wheat. The small farmers were the principal victims of such practices. The kings tried to defend them, while at the same time relying on them in order to preserve the powers of the crown, but the kings did not succeed. The lack of an administrative machinery put local authority back into the hands of the gentry and paralyzed the monarch. This lack of royal power was the result of the rise of Parliament, representing an alliance between the petty and middle nobility and the middle class.

On the continent, for the most part, the aristocracy's attitude was very different. In France, for instance, instead of behaving like agricultural entrepreneurs, the nobles on the whole abandoned the exploitation of land in return for rents paid with money or its equivalent in kind. The large domains were thus divided into small plots, each cultivated by a peasant who had actual control of it. Thus the seigniorial revenues came not from the sale of products on the market but from rents. The peasants gained a certain amount of autonomy in the pursuit of their farming, but agriculture remained largely unaffected by capitalist techniques. There was no alliance between the rural aristocracy and the urban middle class. On the contrary, when the nouveaux riches of the upper middle class bought land from the impoverished nobles they usually exploited it in the same way, in line with their tendency to become assimilated into the nobility.

21

This behavior of the French nobles contributed substantially to their loss of power. In the first place, the rents collected from the peasants, in the framework of an agriculture that remained primitive, were smaller than the revenues that could have been realized from land worked in a modern fashion, that is, by capitalist methods. Thus the middle aristocracy grew poorer in France while it grew richer in Britain. Its potential for resisting the king was thus reduced. In the second place, the rents paid in money or in kind were more and more resented by the peasants. With the reestablishment of public order and the end of civil conflicts and invasions, the aristocracy everywhere had ceased to render the protective services that had been its reason for existing. In Britain it performed new services by transforming and modernizing agriculture. In France it did not do this; as a result it became a parasitic class without real usefulness, and gradually it came to be looked on as such.

Political and cultural factors accentuated the differences in development between the British Parliament and the continental assemblies. In France, for example, the king succeeded very early in obtaining from the Estates General a permanent grant of subsidies to maintain the standing army needed for the defense of the country. He thus acquired an instrument that allowed him to largely free himself from the supervision of the assembly. In Great Britain, whose insular position made her less vulnerable to foreign invasion, Parliament could refuse any such permanent subsidies. The only permanent army was the navy, which could not be used in civil conflicts. The need to secure the authorization of the two Houses for the collection of new taxes forced the king to convene Parliament regularly to obtain the funds required to run the state. Thus the permanence of the Parliament became a necessity.

Yet one should not exaggerate the importance of this factor. The British king had at his disposal large revenues derived from Britain's thriving maritime trade, whereas the trade revenues available to the continental monarchs were not nearly so substantial. Nevertheless the subsidies voted by Parliament represented only a small part of the public wealth. In 1589, after the defeat of the Spanish Armada, the House of Commons authorized only £88,000 of the much larger sum needed to run the country. By not voting the king substantial revenues, Parliament maintained a large measure of control over the monarchy.

Legal theories, closely linked with tradition and cultural values, also played an important role in the effacement of the continental assemblies and the growth of the British Parliament. In France the use of Roman law by the lawyers who surrounded the crown encouraged both national independence and absolutism. The king was considered to be "emperor in his own kingdom." In Great Britain, however, the concept of the common law—the complex of practices, precedents, and specific judicial decisions that serve as references for deciding, by analogy, similar cases—led in the opposite direction. While in France the lawyers reached the conclusion that "whatever is pleasing to the king is law," a conclusion that became the basis of absolute monarchy on the continent, in Britain the concept of the common law held that the king legislates only to complement and interpret the law rather than to change it. Custom, as embodied in the common law, took precedence over everything, even the king; and the existence and powers of Parliament were considered part of the common law. Thus the crown could not assume a legislative sovereignty and use it without the consent of Parliament or in order to get rid of it. When Parliament invoked the common law against the crown, it received considerable support from the people. But in France and on the rest of the continent the idea that there were "fundamental laws of the kingdom" had been destroyed by royal prerogatives.

The development of the British Parliament as a counterweight to royal power eventually resulted in the regime we call a limited monarchy. The king remained the head of state and of the government, and he possessed all the powers that had not been explicitly delegated to other authorities by the common law, tradition, or statute. He was obliged in particular to respect the autonomy of the courts and the prerogatives of the Houses of Parliament. The latter voted funds and deliberated on public affairs. They could vote on proposals that the king submitted to them. They could likewise address petitions to the king, who began to show them more and more consideration.

In the second half of the seventeenth century a different type of evolution manifests itself and begins to develop side by side with the one already described. It is no longer a matter of Parliament's taking over the royal prerogatives but rather a matter of Parliament's replacing the king with a new executive organ: in other words, Parliament radically changes the political regime. At its very height a limited monarchy is being transformed into a parliamentary monarchy in which government is in the hands of a cabinet with a prime minister in charge, holding power only as long as they have the confidence of the legislature or, more precisely, of the House of Commons, whose supremacy over the House of Lords is established by virtue of the fact that it represents the classes that hold economic power.

The principle of the responsibility of government to the House of Commons originated in the criminal proceedings known as impeachment, that is, an accusation for high treason calling for a judgment by the House of Lords acting as the superior court. The example of the Earl of Stafford, executed for treason in 1641, during the years of the conflict between Parliament and Charles I, led his successors to resign rather than face impeachment and the executioner. This rule of ministerial accountability to the Commons seems to have been accepted by the end of the seventeenth century. But its application was not clearcut. It took the form of what French political writers later called "Orleanist Parliamentarism"—the regime that governed in France between 1830 and 1848 under the dynasty of Louis Philippe d'Orleans. According to it ministers cannot govern without the confidence of the Commons, but they must also have the confidence of the king, who can dismiss them without a vote against them in the House. This last qualification gradually disappeared and the ministers came to constitute a team under the authority of the prime minister, who became the real head of the executive, replacing the king. It is at this point that the parliamentary regime was established.

This parliamentary system was not very democratic. At the end of the eighteenth century only 250,000 Britons elected the members of the House of Commons—in other words, barely one-fifth of the men of voting age. The depopulated old medieval towns known as the "rotten boroughs" and the tiny districts created by royal prerogative accounted for a good part of the representation, while the new cities—such as Birmingham and Manchester—had no delegates. Old Sarum, in which there were five dwellings, elected two members. In Dunwich, which had been wiped out when a cliff collapsed, the single property-owner elected himself to the Commons (after, it was said, he had rowed across the submerged borough in a boat). The use of the open ballot aggravated these abuses. The practice of patronage—the support of candidates by great lords or by the crown—made it possible to put in the Commons many of the king's privy councilors and the lords' men.

The parliamentary oligarchy that had thus been created tended to consider itself sovereign with respect to the people as well as the king. Edmund Burke maintained that the members of Parliament, chosen for their good sense and their knowledge of public affairs, had the right to make decisions for themselves, without concern for the will of their electors. He rebuked his electors harshly because they told him how they wanted him to vote. Parliament succeeded even in prohibiting publication of its proceedings in order to protect its members from any direct control by the people. The Wilkes affair (John Wilkes was a journalist who denounced these practices and who was three times thrown out of or deprived of entry into the Commons) was typical: the king and Parliament joined forces against him.

In spite of all this, on the eve of the American and French Revolutions Britain was the only large country in the West in which political institutions were based on election rather than on heredity, even though the elections were very limited and hereditary status retained great influence, both direct (by means of the crown and the House of Lords) and indirect (through patronage, the rotten boroughs, corruption, and so on). The Parliament of Westminster succeeded little by little in erecting round itself a political system that would serve as a model for the plutodemocracies of the nineteenth and twentieth centuries. It was a veritable Trojan horse of plutodemocracy.

Chapter Two
Liberal Ideology and the New Legitimacy

By the eighteenth century British parliamentary institutions and capitalism had become fully rooted in England, but they were still closer to aristo-monarchical patterns than to modern egalitarian, democratic patterns. Throughout the West, rationalist and egalitarian ideologies had made tremendous advances since the development of cities and the market economy: the voyages of discovery and the expansion of the known world, the intellectual and scientific renaissance, and the reform of religion. But these ideologies were at odds with the system of traditional values, based on the authority of the king and the prestige of the nobility, which was still dominant. It was only in the North American colonies that liberalism was more vigorously developed; but these colonies were not independent and they could hardly influence Europe.

Between, roughly, 1787 and 1830—that is, between the writing of the United States Constitution and the simultaneous revolutions in Paris, Vienna, Budapest, Berlin and Warsaw—liberal ideologies gained many adherents, though they did not achieve dominance in the West. The traditional system of values had not lost its influence; in many countries, in fact, it still prevailed. But new ideas had spread everywhere. Belief was rapidly fading in the privileges of birth, in the sacred character of kingship, in the hierarchic, corporate society, in community and reciprocal obligations; rather people were turning to belief in the equality of man, the freedom of thought, free enterprise, national sovereignty, private competition, property and profit. Parliaments, ministerial responsibility, and elections were no longer extraordinary, abnormal phenomena to be found only in a few isolated places: many people everywhere regarded them as reasonable and normal. Pluto-democracy was gaining more and more legitimacy. This was undoubtedly the fundamental reason for its expansion in the years that followed, approximately 1830 to 1870.

The Initial Elements of Liberal Ideology

In general the development of liberal ideology took place in two phases and at very different rhythms. Some elements of liberalism first appeared within the system of aristocratic and monarchical values. These gradually gained strength over the course of several centuries. Other elements of liberal ideology did not appear until the eighteenth century, when they were accepted fairly quickly. Then a kind of crystallization took place: all the elements fitted together, just as water suddenly becomes ice at the freezing point. The evolution of the whole was obviously determined by the forces of production and the structures they generated. Every ideology, every system of values—and the two terms are used synonymously—reflects more or less the needs of the society that it purports to justify.

The interdependence of the two types of phenomena—the slowly evolving elements and the more quickly accepted elements—is, however, complex. The overthrow of the legal order and the triumph of liberal ideology generally coincide with the Industrial Revolution (1780-1830), which made them inevitable. But the cultural revolution that provided a new system of values came somewhat before the Industrial Revolution, at the end of the seventeenth century and throughout the eighteenth. Some of the elements of liberal ideology that appeared in the midst of aristo-monarchical system corresponded to the development of industry and commerce and the emergence of the bourgeoisie. Many of them, however, were latent in the existing structure of values.

The resistance of the nobility to royal power was the first opening for liberal ideology. By affirming that the monarch should rely upon the consensus of his vassals in order to govern, the nobility was championing the idea of elections and representation that liberalism advocates. To affirm that the power of the throne is not hereditary but stems from elections—a principle that the nobility supported and was able to impose in Poland and in the Holy Roman Empire—was equivalent to placing the elective principle above that of hereditary right and ecclesiastic sanctions. This affirmation ushered in one of the cardinal principles of political liberalism. At the same time, the rivalry between the king and the feudal lords led to the development of the theory of limited government, in which the power of the sovereign is qualified by counterweights. The liberals took up this theory and adapted it to their interests, just as they did with the feudal theory and practice of representation.

The role of the church in monarchical societies opened other avenues for the affirmation of liberal ideology. The notion of a natural right, superior to all laws and governmental decisions and binding all, was shaped by the religious authorities in order to limit, for their own advantage, the power of the secular authorities. The modern theory of the limitation of the state by law is directly derived from this. Later Protestantism provided a strong impetus to the development of liberal ideology by ending the authoritarian, hierarchic interpretation of the divine will by the bishops and the pope and replacing it with the principle of freedom of conscience and free inquiry. To lay down the rule that no man can force his interpretation on another was to make the freedom and equality of every man not only the foundation of society but the expression of the divine will itself.

Indeed, the very division of Christendom into a number of denominations—Catholics, Lutherans, Calvinists, Anglicans, and the various other Protestant sects—fostered also liberal ideology by undermining the concept of a single absolute truth. Religious wars shed much blood, occasioned much destruction, inflicted much suffering and horror. But they contributed to the evolution of the idea of the necessity for conflicting doctrines to coexist. Religious pluralism hastened the birth of political pluralism.

Even more important, as Max Weber argued in *The Protestant Ethic and the Spirit of Capitalism*, Protestantism in its Puritan form favored the development of economic liberalism by developing an ethic that corresponded to capitalism. In a religious doctrine based on predestination, where nobody knows if he is one of the "elect" or one of "the damned," success through hard work becomes a sign of divine election that reassures the believer and saves him from doubt and anxiety. The humble fisherman to whom Luther promised grace is replaced by the confident, steel-faced merchants of the heroic days of capitalism. However, although the believer ought to seek material success—in an industrial and commercial society, in other words, the greatest possible profit—he should not enjoy his wealth and profits. Hence the Protestant ethic is in total accord with capitalism, which exalts the search for maximum profit and at the same time the reinvestment of the largest part of this profit in production. Because their religion had led certain Western groups to adopt so unnatural a behavior—to labor doggedly for the greatest possible amount of money not in order to benefit by it but in order to earn still more, and so on—they were able to carry the logic of capitalism to its ultimate end.

Protestantism's structure, more than its doctrine, contributed to its adaptation to capitalism and encouraged liberal ideology. After the Counter-Reformation, the Catholic Church, founded on the authority of the pope, the hierarchy of the bishops, centralization and rigorous obedience to official dogma imposed from above, resembled the monarchic and aristocratic secular society, which itself reflected an agrarian, paternalist, rigid civilization. The Protestant sects, established as autonomous communities, each composed of believers with equal rights, freely debating the meaning of the word of God, collectively governing their parishes with the help of a minister who functioned through persuasion rather than edict, were like little republics and, at the same time, like business enterprises—in other words, the two basic models of plutodemocracy. These models evolved on the religious level before they spread into the economic and political sphere.

The major components of liberal ideology had existed for some time before they were synthesized into a body of doctrine, a coherent system of values: equality, freedom of thought, pluralism, competition and freedom of enterprise, profit-making, respect for wealth and material success. The discovery of the New World, with its different civilizations, shattered the idea of a single social order in the world and strengthened the idea of relativity. Renaissance humanism enhanced the scientific and critical spirit and suggested new institutional and cultural models drawn from antiquity. The renewed interest in the Greeks and Romans during the Renaissance revived the ideas of the citizen, the republic, the national community, freedom, and equality. The Roman concept of property offered capitalism a legal instrument better suited to it than the feudal notion of multiple rights superimposed on a single estate and restricted by collective interests and "service."

In the early part of the eighteenth century these elements were often still ambiguous. They were embedded in an overall view of the world that was still inspired by aristocratic ideology. Therefore, the first syntheses of liberal ideas, naturally had the same ambiguity: they were gestating the new liberal ideology, but also serving to rejuvenate and modify the aristocratic ideology. Montesquieu's ideas are an excellent illustration of this situation: he developed a theory of a monarchy limited by representative assemblies in which the nobility, coming from the upper middle class, would have a considerable place.

Physiocracy[1] is another transitional ideology. Stressing that land is only a source of wealth, that it provides only a net increment, the Physiocrats obviously vindicated the landed aristocracy at the very moment when economic changes were against it. But the Physiocrats' conception of land was totally different from the conception of land in feudal ideology. They did not see in land a base of political power, a means of buttressing the nobility, or a complex of mutual rights and obligations, but simply a factor of production and profit. For them land was capital. In this sense they promoted capitalism among the land-owners and pushed the French aristocracy in the same general direction followed by the British nobility a long time before. Through means different than those imputed to Calvin by Max Weber, the Physiocrats came to the same conclusions regarding agriculture.

Can we regard enlightened despotism as a transitional ideology? To a large extent, no. Important philosophers of the eighteenth century such as Voltaire and Diderot hoped that the kings they flattered would use their power to impose liberal reforms, such as freedom of the press or religious toleration. In fact only one, Joseph II of Germany, tried it—without success. Physiocrats like Mercier de la Riviére and Turgot thought that the royal power could be used to break down the obstacles to increased economic production. Here again the facts did not accord with the theory. In truth, the doctrine of enlightened despotism is only an ideological cover for absolute monarchy. But it appeared at a time when it was already outmoded, made obsolete by social developments. Napoleon I would use it a few decades later in a new form by

1. Physiocracy—the rule of nature—was a French school of the mid-eighteenth century that looked to a society in which natural economic law would govern and positive—that is, man-made—law would be in harmony with natural law. It was the Physiocrats who conceived the slogan, *"Laissez faire, laissez passer."*—Translator.

combining elements of political absolutism with republican principles (equality, universal suffrage, free enterprise). In fact, Bonapartism is the only form of enlightened despotism ever really put into effect. It shaped the elements of the Western system that the bourgeoisie needed at the very moment when this class was in danger of being submerged by the masses in the context of liberal institutions. In this respect, it can be considered a transitional ideology, but it appeared after the cultural revolution of the eighteenth century that was to synthesize the various elements of liberal thought into a coherent system.

The Cultural Revolution of the Eighteenth Century

In a matter of a few decades in the eighteenth century, a generation of thinkers put the various components of liberalism together in the form of a coherent and grandiose synthesis. This spread throughout the whole of the West a new conception of man and society, a new vision of the world, a new system of values that called for institutions radically different from those of the ancien régime. The first thrust for this development came from the English Civil War undertaken by Cromwell, which challenged radically the existing order. Milton and his "republic of the believers," George Fox and his Quakers, John Lilburne and his Levellers developed a theory of a society without nobles and without kings. But the center of the "cultural earthquake" was France, at the time a dominant power, where we find a remarkable team of intellectuals, notably Rousseau, Diderot, d'Alembert, and Condorcet. The new ideology they expounded expresses the interests and the aspirations of the Western bourgeoisie at the dawn of the expansion of capitalism. Its remarkable power of attraction stems from the fact that it favors the liberation of all men, including those exploited by plutodemocracy. Equality, liberty, popular sovereignty, elections—these principles have universal appeal.

The term "cultural revolution" is wholly accurate, for the old ideology came under attack in all its aspects and in its very foundations. Equality was opposed to privilege and hierarchy; freedom of thought and expression was opposed to the principles enforced by popes and kings; economic competition was opposed to the immobility of the corporative system and "the eternal order of the fields"; individualism was opposed to communitarian concepts; the quest for profit was

31

opposed to the prestige of birth and feudal ideas of service. The existing order lost *all* justification. If men were free and equal, no one could command them unless he had received their mandate to do so: that was the deathblow for the monarchy and led to elective republics. The authority of the priests and the nobles was similarly undermined. Thus we witness a real emancipation of humankind, which finally comes of age by freeing itself of political and social forces modeled on the image of the father.

The cultural revolution was far more shattering in the Catholic countries. Protestantism had prepared the minds of the people in Protestant countries through its doctrine of free inquiry and its acceptance of material success. As a result, the reversal of values in these countries took place without turmoil, and the opposition between religion and the new doctrine was not great. We must not forget, however, that Lutheranism very often led to a spiritual domination that was not much less potent than that of Rome. Nor should we forget that Puritanism often produced intolerant regimes, for example in Massachusetts, where only the members of the church had the right to vote and where dissidents were persecuted and exiled.

The new ideology assumed the proportions of a propaganda movement in the French and the American Revolutions, to which it contributed and by which it was reinforced. At the beginning the revolt of the thirteen American colonies against England did not involve a struggle of one system against another. Their institutions were very much like those of Great Britain, and democracy was hardly more advanced in the colonies than in the mother country. The powers of the legislatures vis-à-vis the governors were similar to those of the British Parliament vis-à-vis the king. The franchise was equally restricted on both sides of the Atlantic, except for Rhode Island, where all the married males could vote. To be sure, there were no nobles in America and the bourgeois and capitalist spirit was far more prevalent there. But the colonists were not fighting against the British nobility. It was the commercial rivalry with the British firms that was the basic source of the conflict: it was a conflict between two bourgeoisies and two capitalisms.

However, once the conflict started it had to be given an ideology capable of uniting all the colonists and transforming the struggle into a political conflict. The principles of the cultural revolution that the European philosophers had elaborated provided the only possible political platform that corresponded at the same time to the social structure and the egalitarian conceptions of the colonists. The publication of *Common Sense* by Tom Paine, on January 10, 1776, led the American Revolution in this direction. Paine called for an egalitarian republic in which all citizens participate in public affairs and in which they all designate their representatives in frequent elections that guarantee the representatives' loyalty to the common welfare. Six months later the Declaration of Independence proclaimed the same ideas in a solemn document that transformed the ideas of the cultural revolution into a plan for political action. It put tremendous emphasis on nationalism, and the Declaration's ringing assertion that a nation is a society of equal men united by their collective will and not by feudal ties or by loyalty to a king became an essential element of liberalism. The struggle of the thirteen colonies for their independence became the struggle of a new liberal society against the old aristocracies and monarchies.

In this manner the new ideology acquired an international dimension. The entire West was involved. The fact that a nineteen-year-old French aristocrat—Lafayette—enlisted on the side of the Americans attested to the impression made by the event on the far side of the Atlantic. Lafayette's action had the same significance as Byron's later in Greece, or André Malraux's during the Spanish Civil War, or Régis Debray's in Bolivia. Thus the victory of the colonists became the triumph of liberal ideology. The republican constitution that the Americans adopted provided the first institutional paradigm that owed nothing to the old monarchist and aristocratic systems. The haven for victims of religious persecution became the land of political freedom and capitalist expansion. A republic was not merely a dream, for now there existed a great republic, prosperous and dynamic.

The model developed in the United States "republicanized" the limited monarchy that had been established in Great Britain at the beginning of the eighteenth century by replacing the king with an elected president and the hereditary peers with an elected Senate. It also embraced a new concept of community life, based on a mixture of religious traditions and economic practices. Citizen participation in collective life was highly developed in the United States because it corresponded to the traditions of the Protestant sects that established the British colonies in America. The moralism and religiosity of social and political life were also associated with these traditions. In addition,

33

administration, municipal organization, and the organization of political life followed the pattern of the commercial enterprises that took part in colonization and later multiplied. Protestant communities and business firms alike constituted little republics whose spirit and methods contributed to shape the great North American republic.

The French Revolution of 1789 did not generate a fully developed republic after the failures of the Jacobin republic and the Directorate. But the impact of the Declaration of the Rights of Man in 1789 was even greater in Europe than that of the Declaration of Independence. For the second time in a few years the new ideology was used as a springboard for political action, proclaimed in a form even more complete and explosive than the American Declaration. Besides being inherently dramatic as a vast revolutionary movement, the French Revolution had a tremendous impact because it took place in the greatest and the oldest nation of Europe. The ten years between 1789 and 1799 created a ferment in Europe. Thereafter monarchy and aristocracy were outmoded and severely weakened.

The wars of the Revolution and the French Empire contributed a great deal to the propagation of liberal ideology. Whatever his private motives, Napoleon Bonaparte was in effect that fighter for the Rights of Man that he described in his memoirs, posing for history. He carried revolutionary ideas everywhere, even though he ruled as a dictator, restored a monarchy, and created a new aristocracy. In spite of crown and consecration he was still an upstart. The imperial nobility was composed principally of other upstarts, and its titles conferred no power: it amounted to a kind of hereditary honorary society. Napoleon's armies overturned thrones, or caused them to rock. They degraded nobles and priests. They humiliated the pope. Everywhere they introduced the Civil Code of law, founded on equality of birth and capitalist ownership.

In 1815, after the exile of Napoleon, the Congress of Vienna was to endeavor in vain to revive the old legitimacy. After the twenty-five years of war and revolution that had so deeply shaken the aristo-monarchical system, no populace believed in it any longer except those in backward rural areas under the thumb of the church. These areas were still numerous, but in a world in which industry was growing with great strides, they no longer determined the development of society. The armies of the Holy Alliance were powerless to stop the evolution of liberal ideology, which represented the new legitimacy. Louis-Lépold Boilly's two drawings—*The Liberal* and *The Ultra* (that is, the extremist conservative)—were symbolic. The first is smiling because the future belongs to him; the second is sad because it is fleeing from him. In the half-century that followed the Congress of Vienna, plutodemocracy spread throughout the West.

Chapter Three

Resistance, Revolution, and Class Conflict

The triumph of the Western system did not come about without conflict and violence. The possessors of political power, the kings, the nobles, and their allies, did not allow themselves to be deprived of it without a fight. They employed every possible means of coercion to withstand the pressure of their opponents. The propagation of liberal ideas had long been hampered by strict censorship supported by the religious authorities, especially in Catholic countries. Representative assemblies were often broken up by armed men, and their leaders were hunted down, imprisoned, and even executed. The advocates of the new order, for their part, had occasionally resorted to force, attacking noblemen's castles or royal palaces in peasant and urban risings. The development of the liberal system evolved after a long and implacable conflict marked by phases of calm and storm.

The revolution of the seventeenth century in England and the American and French Revolutions of the eighteenth century are the most important rebellions in this long conflict, but they were not the first. Since the Middle Ages there had been revolutionary movements: urban uprisings, such as those of the French merchants under Etienne Marcel; peasant revolts in France and Germany, religious wars that had a social character; and so on. They were followed by other intense conflicts. Immediately after the Congress of Vienna the militia of the Holy Alliance intervened in a number of countries to crush liberal revolutions. In 1830 revolutionary uprisings became stronger and more widespread, bringing parliamentary regimes to France and Belgium. In 1848 Western Europe was submerged by a revolutionary wave that totally destroyed the French monarchy. In 1871 the Commune of Paris was broken by one of the bloodiest repressions the West had known in the nineteenth century.

The preceding sketch of events takes into account only the major movements that shook or crumbled the established systems. It omits a mass of conspiracies, clandestine and overt risings, agitations of every kind that were harshly repressed by the established governments. It also leaves out the revolutions and guerrilla wars of Latin America, which could not result in the establishment of liberal governments because of lack of the appropriate economic and social infrastructure: these were agrarian nations, under- or semi-developed economically and technically, and hence not ripe for plutodemocracy. Nevertheless, their battles for independence were part of the great campaign against the established monarchies.

These revolutionary movements that helped to establish the liberal system can be grouped in two categories. Until 1848 they were aimed essentially against the nobility, the kings, and their allies—in other words, against the champions of the old order. The barricades of June 1848 in France and the repression that smashed them opened a new phase. The old ruling classes were no longer the major obstacles to the development of plutodemocracy; they were replaced by the new oppressed class, the proletariat, which was beginning to become sufficiently powerful to threaten capitalism. To schematize, one might say that before 1848 the middle class was fighting on a single front and that after 1848 it fought on two fronts, the newer of which soon became more important than the older.

The Struggle against the Defenders of Aristo-Monarchy

The Marxist theory of class struggle was primarily elaborated to explain the conflict between the ancien régime and the contemporary Western system. It provided an explanatory scheme to account for the latter. In general, Marxism holds, the traditional monarchy expressed the interest of the aristocracy, while plutodemocracy expressed the interest of the bourgeoisie. However, neither the aristocracy nor the bourgeoisie are homogeneous, clearly defined classes. They both include different groups and categories. At the same time people do not always have a political attitude that is compatible with the interests of their class, either because they are not conscious of their interests or because they reject them for idealistic reasons. In other words, class identification is not always clear. The interests of the same class are at times contradictory and the individuals do not always espouse the interests of their class.

To say, therefore, that a political system is the expression of social class is not to say that a class as a whole accepts or makes the system. The Marxists believe, for instance, that a working-class party is a working-class party because it defends the objective interests of the workers even if the majority of the workers do not support it because they are not class-conscious. In fact the dominant classes always try to arrest the development of the class-consciousness of the workers in order to weaken them. They thus try, often successfully, to make those they dominate accept the status quo and act against their own interests. The struggles against the aristo-monarchy associated with the development of the Western system provide many examples of this phenomenon.

This conflict involves not exploiter and exploited, but the dominant class of the traditional agrarian system and the dominant class in a capitalist economy. However, the oppressed classes become involved as plutodemocracy gives them more effective means of resistance (elections, liberties, working class parties, trade unions, public education, and so on) and as liberal ideology expresses certain universal values (liberty, equality, and popular sovereignty). One can therefore understand why the people supported the bourgeoisie despite the fact that they were exploited by it in the Marxist sense of the term. The workers before 1850 established an alliance with the bourgeoisie very similar to the one advocated today by the Communist parties in the underdeveloped world in their struggle against the big landowners and foreign capitalism.

It is less understandable that the aristocracy was supported by the peasants, who could not possibly find any hope of emancipation in the old political system. Their motives are baffling. The nobility made use of religion, especially in Catholic countries, to reinforce the peasants' emotional attachment to the established order. The idea that this order was natural and that its destruction would lead to anarchy aroused a deep response among the peasants. They were ready to believe that this order was the will of God, like the order of the seasons, of crops, of life and death. The priests' teachings sustained these beliefs, creating a barrier to the penetration of liberal ideas. The farmer's resentment against the townsman, aggravated by a sullen jealousy and a feeling of inferiority, reinforced the peasants' alliance with the landed aristocracy. This alliance, of course, did not exist everywhere. In a number of parts of Europe there were liberal and even revolutionary peasant movements.

Other social categories also neglected their class interests in favor of noneconomic considerations. The children of the privileged classes—or, more precisely, their leaders—often embraced such an attitude, as previously mentioned—Lafayette and Byron were aristocrats who deliberately embraced the liberal cause, and Malraux and Debray were bourgeois who deliberately embraced the socialist cause. The "Fayettists" and the young liberal noblemen played an important part in France in 1789, just as their leader had done ten years earlier in America.

Both friends and enemies of plutodemocracy constituted relatively heterogeneous groups that have never precisely coincided with the middle class or the aristocracy. If "class" is the clue to the conflict between the liberal and the monarchist systems, it leads along an obscure and tortuous path. Nonetheless, the class struggle tended to become more clearly delineated as the interests of the contending parties were more clearly differentiated and as they became more self-conscious. Thus a certain development may be traced through the revolutions that mark the evolution of plutodemocracy.

The seventeenth-century English revolution was certainly the most complex and the most ambiguous. To reduce it to a conflict between the Cavaliers, representing the aristocracy, and the Roundheads, representing the middle class, is to oversimplify it. Rural nobles and the middle class had long been drawn close together by a capitalist type of production, and both tended to support Parliament against the king. Not all of them rallied to Cromwell, nor did all the great lords devoted to the feudal system align themselves with the crown. Each group was more or less divided. In this case religious differences were probably more important than class conflicts, and local rivalries also played a large part.

The American Revolution was a war of liberation rather than a class conflict. But these two phenomena are generally linked. The national movements in Europe in 1830 and 1848 and those of Latin America in the same period represent forms of the struggle of the liberal bourgeoisies against the dominant aristocracies. The revolt of the thirteen colonies against England has some of the same characteristics, even though England already had a parliamentary regime and even though the major factor was the rivalry between American and British capitalists.

Class conflict was not absent in the American Civil War, which comes closer to being a revolution of class against class. True, a genuine nobility was not strong in the South, though some planters were descended from Cavaliers; but the structure of the great estates, their exploitation by slave labor, the local customs and the way of life were all aristocratic in type. The North, in contrast, was the embodiment of industrial capitalism, and the West was agrarian lower-middle class, egalitarian, and Puritanical; certain approximate equivalents could be found in some parts of Europe, where they were to give birth to liberal peasant parties, for example, in Scandinavia and Switzerland. In short, the "classes" in the United States took on a regional aspect: the Civil War did not set social groups from the same territory against each other; rather it pitted states with one social structure against others with a different one.

The French Revolution of 1789 came closest to being a class conflict. It set the aristocracy against the middle class in its initial phase. The division of the Estates General into "orders"—clergy, nobility, Third Estate—enhanced the cleavage. The ecclesiastics soon divided into two groups. The bishops, all of whom were aristocrats, joined the nobility. Most of the priests and curates joined the Third Estate. Thus it was possible to describe the whole as a "national assembly," inasmuch as it represented virtually the entire nation. The emigration of the aristocrats, who began to flee abroad in 1790, opened the second phase. Under the Convention, the conflict was waged between factions of the middle class: the Girondist upper middle class against the Jacobin middle bourgeoisie, which subsequently had to battle the working-class *enragés* (the angry ones). In the beginning the Paris revolution of 1830 was a continuation of the class struggle between the aristocracy and the middle class. At first only a few aristocrats made common cause with the middle class, under the same man who had led them forty-one years earlier: Lafayette. But gradually many more noblemen flocked to Lafayette's cause. The French nobility had begun to participate in capitalism and it wished to become part of it. Louis-Philippe was their man, as he was that of the bankers, the industrialists, and the tradesmen. The trend in revolutionary struggles of a fairly clear-cut conflict between the bourgeoisie and aristo-monarchy was beginning to change.

The Resistance to Popular Movements and Nascent Socialism

The French revolution of 1848 was a turning point in the development of plutodemocracy. At first it was a revolution similar to those that had preceded it, representing the struggle of the middle class against the aristocracy. Both, however, had changed considerably and both were torn by internal conflicts. Part of the traditional aristocracy had undertaken an "internal emigration," shutting itself into its town houses in the Faubourg St.-Germain, sunk in bitter recollections of the past. The rest had enlisted in the ranks of capitalism alongside the upper-middle-class industrialists, merchants, and speculators. What the British nobility had done at the close of the Middle Ages, these aristocrats now did. The new ruling class thus created wanted to preserve its financial, political, and electoral privileges (there were two hundred thousand voters in a population of thirty million). Against them there were arrayed the middle and lower middle classes, determined to have equality. In February 1848 they made an alliance with the workers in order to establish the republic and universal suffrage.

Between 1830 and 1848 a great number of peasants from the countryside moved into the cities looking for work. Many could not find jobs because the number of peasants exceeded by far the number of jobs available. Those who did find work lived under the most abominable conditions: the working day was twelve to fourteen hours, wages were extremely low, housing conditions were dreadful (several families would be lodged in a single cellar at exorbitant rents), children of six or eight had to go to work in order to keep their families alive, women had to take jobs or become prostitutes, shop discipline was like that of a prison or a concentration camp, and so on. Employers' good will or charity was useless in the prevailing competitive conditions. Anyone who treated his employees decently would incur higher production costs that would doom him to bankruptcy. Such circumstances were not peculiar to France. They were to be found in every country that was industrializing—in other words, in all the large Western nations. One must not forget this nineteenth-century condition if one hopes to

41

understand Marx. It constitutes the very foundation of his doctrine. In fact, he made a remarkable analysis of it. It was not pure chance that *The Communist Manifesto* appeared a few months before the 1848 French revolution: both were the products of the same conditions.

But in spite of the dynamism of industry and the growth of the cities, agriculture was still dominant. The proletariat was still too weak to be able to impose its views, the more so because it had little schooling, almost no training, and hardly any organization. But it had become powerful enough to be an ally worth having. In February of 1848, it helped the middle class to overthrow the last remains of the aristo-monarchy—in other words, to eliminate the throne, to establish the republic, to institute universal suffrage, to proclaim public freedoms. These reforms, which satisfied the desires of its allies, were also helpful to it, but they were certainly not enough. The right to form trade unions, the right to strike, the right to form political parties, freedom of association and mass protest, free elections, universal suffrage—all these were useful to the workers. But they would not be satisfied with them: guaranteed employment, fair wages, fair working conditions, and job security were basic, urgent demands. Unless they were met, political freedoms would remain merely "formal," as Marx put it.

Thus, after February 1848, France was the only big republic in Europe, the only country with universal suffrage, the only place where some basic civil liberties had been granted; but liberalism was only shakily established and many more reforms were needed before liberalism could become firmly entrenched. The desire for more social reform prompted the middle class to continue its alliance with the proletariat. Steps in this direction included the presence of a worker in the republican provisional government of 1848 and the actions of the Luxembourg Committee, a group created by the provisional government under the direction of two of its members and comprising 657 workers elected by different craft organizations, 231 employers, and a number of authors. Named for its meeting place in the Luxembourg Gardens, the committee adopted some important regulations, including the reduction of the working day to ten hours in Paris and eleven hours in the provinces. The tendency toward reform was embodied in men like the poet Alphonse Lamartine and the lawyer Alexandre Ledru-Rollin, and it led to bringing the lower middle class and the proletariat closer together, as Robespierre had done, in order to form a party that would oppose the party created by the alliance of the upper middle class with the nobles who had opted for capitalism; the struggle between the two would take place in the context of plutodemocracy. In order to win over to its cause the artisans, the small shopkeepers, the small peasants, and all the other members of the lower classes who might feel sympathetic to the workers and join them in an alliance of the poor against the rich, the "party of order" drove the proletariat to revolt. This was the effect of the decree that ordered the closing of the "National Workshops," which had been created by the provisional government to prevent unemployment, and threw four hundred thousand Parisians out of work. They flung up barricades and launched a civil war. In this conflict, known as the June Days of 1848, the army gained the day for the "party of order," which was supported by the lower middle class and the peasantry.

The same mechanism was to go into operation again in France twenty-three years later. In 1871, when Thiers's government evacuated Paris after a neighborhood riot that was easy to quell, it left the capital entirely in the hands of the workers; they set up an insurrectional commune—the Paris Commune. The city was then taken by the army, street by street, in fierce fighting, and the frightening repression that followed (twenty to thirty thousand summary executions) broke the spirit of socialism for a long time to come, while the recollection of civil war struck panic into the whole middle class from lower to upper, as well as the aristocracy. Thus the proletariat was cut off from the artisans, the shopkeepers, and the small farmers, who were thereby prevented from posing a serious threat to the plutodemocratic system. On the contrary, they helped it to grow: fear of the "Reds"—the revolutionaries—continued, as it had done in June 1848, to reconcile the former antagonists in earlier class conflicts.

Thus the character of the conflict between classes changed. In simple terms, it was no longer a conflict between the nobility and the bourgeoisie but between the proletariat of the towns and an alliance of the nobles, the bourgeois, and the peasants. The aristocracy and the bourgeoisie, formerly opponents, began to collaborate within an expanding capitalistic system in which the aristocracy found in business affairs and politics a compensation for its lost privileges. Between capitalists and workers, however, the conflict of interests did not diminish at all. But the workers were too weak to confront a block formed by the bourgeoisie, the peasants, and the nobility except in occasional outbursts such as strikes and riots.

Yet the development of the liberal system progressively reinforced the position of the proletariat. The growth of capitalism led to an increased demand for workers and the development of their education and political consciousness. The new regime allowed them new weapons: working-class parties, trade unions, popular newspapers, and electoral and parliamentary platforms. But this same evolution integrated the workers into the system and weakened their revolutionary ardor. The improvement of their living conditions accentuated this trend. The same is true with democratic procedures. "Elections—Treason"—this slogan of the French leftists in May 1968 is not wholly without basis. The right to vote and the debates and actions of the legislature give a sense of participation that is often quite illusory, but yet effective in stifling real political activity. Social demands, if made and met in this manner, tend to bolster the status quo rather than transform it.

In the United States the integration of the proletariat within the Western system was almost complete by around 1870. In Europe at the same time socialism had become a system with values that rivaled the liberal ideology and that was supported by large popular groups. But they often took a reformist and legal stance, as in Great Britain. Even when they claimed to be revolutionary, they were so more in words than in acts, and as their power increased they used it to make liberal democracy more acceptable to the workers.

Thus arose the conditions that allow the Western system to function. Its political institutions are based on the notion that the political parties chosen to govern by the vote of the citizens will respect political pluralism, will never use their power to destroy their opponents, and will allow a party elected by the majority to replace them. Such moderation assumes that the conflict of classes is attenuated enough so that the opposing parties can exist together within an established regime that cannot be changed except by legal means. Violent revolution is advocated by so few that the system is not really in danger. This is exactly the situation between 1871 and 1914, when the West did not experience great revolutionary movements such as the ones that shook it in the preceding century.

44

By the beginning of the nineteenth century, then, the Industrial Revolution had destroyed the aristo-monarchical system, which no longer corresponded to the productive forces of capitalism. But it should be noted that capitalism could have been established under political forms other than liberal democracy, for instance, Bonapartism, between 1852 and 1870 or the Fascism of the 1930's. In order for the Western system to develop fully it was necessary for capitalism to coincide with a weakening of class conflict sufficient to allow the development of the general consensus that is indispensable to the functioning of democratic institutions. Such a consensus has existed twice, between 1870 and 1914 and since 1945. The years between the two world wars, 1918-1945, formed an intermediary period. After 1870 two types of the Western system developed, each in close relationship to the development of the forces of production as well as other social structures: first, liberal democracy (1870-1939) discussed in Part II; second, technodemocracy (1945 on), discussed in Part III.

In the second half of the nineteenth century plutodemocracy established itself solidly on both sides of the Atlantic. The starting point for this first burgeoning of the system was approximately 1870. In the United States the victory of the North in the Civil War in 1865 reinforced liberal ideology and capitalism, consolidated the federal union and the central government, and gave its institutions the character that was to survive until the reforms of Franklin D. Roosevelt. Lincoln's accession also marked the crystallization of the Republican and Democratic parties. The South, however, remained outside the realm of liberalism. Although the former slaves now had the right to vote, they could not use it freely. In the Reconstruction period their votes were exploited by men from the North. When a compromise with the federal authorities was worked out, the southern states adopted regulations that deprived the blacks of the right to vote. The Democratic party enjoyed a monopoly of representation in the South that brought the United States closer to a single-party system than to liberal pluralism.

In Western Europe, too, it was the south—Spain, Portugal, Italy—that remained outside plutodemocracy. But in the same period the system was establishing itself little by little almost everywhere else. In Britain, where the defeat of George III's attempt at a restoration of absolute monarchy had consolidated the parliamentary system, the laws of 1832 and 1876 increased the number of voters and led to the formation of organized parties. Parliamentarianism in France evolved slowly between 1814 and 1848, the basis of a very small electorate (one to two hundred thousand voters out of a population of thirty million). The Second Republic instituted universal suffrage in 1848, and it was never to be abolished; but initially it was confined to plebiscites. The Third Republic joined parliamentarianism with universal suffrage: from 1875 on the liberal system functioned in France. Most of the smaller European countries followed the trend, or anticipated it slightly. Sweden adopted a constitution in 1814 and supplanted the old assemblies of estates in 1866 with a parliament whose powers were gradually increased. Belgium had adopted parliamentary government as early as 1831. Denmark and the

Netherlands followed suit in 1848, and in 1866 they broadened the voting base. After 1870 Germany, Austria, and Italy were the only countries among those who practice it today in which plutodemocracy did not exist. Germany, however, did have universal suffrage for national elections.

We call "liberal democracy" the first stage of plutodemocracy because it is based upon individualistic structures that correspond to a great extent to liberal ideology. The political parties consist of persons that do not accept common rules of action, except in England. Every parliamentarian votes as he likes without paying attention to the directions that come from the top. Interest groups are not yet well developed and they, too, have similar individualistic structures. Large working-class formations appear only at the end of the nineteenth century. But until 1914 they remain in opposition and do not affect institutional mechanisms; they represent a sort of counterforce outside of the system. Between 1918 and 1939 mass socialist parties begin to participate in the governments of many countries of Europe—but, as we shall see, this is an intermediary period. Under liberal democracy economic institutions correspond to the political ones. Production and trade are carried on through family firms of unequal sizes. In the United States the size of the country and its relative "youth" account for the development of huge firms, but they generally retain the same individualistic character that produced the "barons" of industry and the great financiers of Europe. Business firms are generally controlled by an individual or a family, and even the trusts, which concentrate great economic power, often retain the same individualistic form. In this period we are still far away from contemporary capitalism, in which the participation of the banks and the large institutions of credit create collective structures. During this period the head of each firm acts as he pleases in the context of a competitive market, without being concerned with state economic plans, rules controlling credit and investments, and collective bargaining.

Liberal democracy was to function in the West without serious problems for almost a half century, until World War I. It coincided with a huge rise in population and substantial urbanization, impressive expansion in industry based on coal and steel, the expansion of the means of communication, a rise in wealth and in economic inequalities—in a word, the expansion of capitalism—though this growth was not uninterrupted, for there were several depressions of varying intensity. The growth of capitalism was accompanied by a decline in religion and a surge of faith in science, an upsurge of nationalism, and an increase in colonial conquest and imperialism. It was a vigorous era, characterized by the upsurge of the economy, science, ideas, and the arts. It was also a peaceful era, marked by the absence of wars and by relatively little domestic violence: private habits became more civilized and the class struggle assumed a less revolutionary character.

The First World War struck liberal economic and political structures hard. After 1914 liberal democracy found itself in a serious crisis, the acuteness of which varied from country to country; but it existed everywhere. The great depression of 1929 made this crisis even deeper and more painful. Capitalism and parliamentarianism seemed to be incapable of meeting the situation. In this transitional period between the two world wars, liberal democracy disintegrated to make way for a new form of plutodemocracy that emerged fully after 1945. This crisis will be examined in a separate chapter, Chapter 6. The aspects of liberal democracy analyzed in Chapters 4 and 5 represent chiefly the period of its expansion from 1870 to 1914.

Chapter Four
Political Organization

The political organization and structure of liberal democracy forms a well-patterned whole. It comprises popular sovereignty, popular elections, legislative assemblies, the independence of the judiciary, civil liberties, and political parties, all of which are complementary to each other and derive from the same fundamental principles. Some of the elements of the aristo-monarchical system remain: the king, in some countries; the upper chamber; the inequalities of representation; restrictions on the right to vote. But they diminish in importance during this period; franchise becomes increasingly universal after World War I, the House of Lords loses most of its powers after the Parliamentary Act of 1911, and so on. In fact, most of those elements of the past retain only a decorative character, like antique sculptures used in modern buildings. Only the inequality of voting persists.

Despite its coherent structure, this political organization does not establish a strong political power. Compared with the strong states of the absolute monarchies, liberal states are weak. This weakness corresponds to the ideology of liberalism, whose political and economic aspects coincide. The desire to weaken the state stems at first from the will to protect the freedoms of the individual against the intervention of the state. Liberal thinking is based on the idea that every power is dangerous by its very nature because those who willed it are likely to abuse it. To liberate the individual it is necessary to weaken the power of the state. And the same is true in order to insure private initiative in industry and commerce, free competition, and capitalism. Every intervention by the state in this area is evil, because it cannot at the same time provide for economic efficiency and satisfy the private enterprises.

One should not, however, exaggerate the weakness of the liberal state. It is less confined than aristo-monarchy by traditional principles and habits and has more freedom of action. It governs with greater efficiency. It was able to win World War I against the empires of central Europe despite their authoritarian character. No doubt, this was due less to the action of the governments than to the advanced technology created by capitalism, but this technology in turn was closely linked to the development of a certain kind of authority within the Western systems. The weakness of the liberal state is only political weakness. Economic power continues to grow and to dominate the state.

Institutions

The institutions of liberal democracy are quite different in the United States and in Europe. The differences are secondary in comparison with these institutions' essential similarity under the plutodemocratic system, but they are nevertheless important. The constitutional pattern is not the same on both sides of the Atlantic. It did not evolve in the same contexts; ways of life, modes of thinking, and cultural patterns are as important as economic conditions in this connection.

The Parliamentary Executive and the Presidential Executive

Before 1914 France was the only parliamentary republic in Europe. After 1918 Germany also adopted a republican system, as did several central European countries, where liberal democracy worked badly (except in Czechoslovakia). With very few exceptions, parliamentary institutions were still based on a monarchy. But the power of the monarch was now a fiction: "the king reigns but does not govern." He was henceforth to be restricted to a symbolic function. The executive power belonged to the cabinet, whose real chief was the prime minister. The cabinet's responsibility to the houses of parliament—or to the house chosen by direct vote of the citizens—became the basic element in the system, except in the United States, where it was unknown, as was the prime minister's power to dissolve the popularly elected chamber.

Such a mechanism seems strange, complicated, fragile. It owes its success in Europe and in the British Commonwealth to the fact that it made possible a smooth and gradual conversion of existing monarchies into plutodemocracies by following the technique of the hermit crab, the crustacean that destroys a mollusk in order to set up housekeeping in its shell. The outer appearance is scarcely altered but the interior is completely changed. The slow evolution that gradually deprived the British monarch of his powers was facilitated by the same sort of process. The system remained monarchical in appearance but became parliamentary in substance. The presidents of France and the United States are essentially democratic transplants of the king of England: the difference in *their* real powers corresponds to the change in his real powers during the nineteenth century.

The parliamentary system met liberal democracy's need to develop in Europe within a monarchist framework. The division of the executive into two components—the head of the state and the head of the government—was intended essentially to limit the king to purely honorific functions and to transfer the real power to a man who came out of the parliament and who was dependent on it. The legislators' right to force the prime minister and his cabinet to resign was intended to prevent the king from being able to choose his government without the parliament's consent. None of this has any significance in the United States, whose break with the mother country was also a break with monarchy.

The problem in the evolution of American institutions was quite different. There was no question of combating a king or a nobility, since they did not exist. The problem was that of weakening the central authority to guarantee the rights of the states. Locke's and Montesquieu's theories of the separation of powers, evolved by their authors to weaken the power of the throne, were transplanted to assure the freedom of action of local governments. The conflict between the Federalists and the Anti-Federalists, which emerged during the early decades of the newly independent government, must not be misconstrued. The opposition was based on the degree of state autonomy, not on the principle itself, which was challenged by no one. Much more than the parliamentary system, the American presidential system is one of checks and balances. The European prime ministers are not the rivals of their parliaments; they come out of them and can govern only in agreement with them. Dissolution of the popularly elected chamber by the prime minister and that chamber's ability to bring down the prime minister's government by a vote of no confidence are the means of restoring the necessary accord between the two powers, not instruments intended to put them on an equal footing in the event of a conflict between them. In the United States, such conflict is normal and constant. The two powers are equal and rivals. Each specializes in its domain—legislative or executive—without impinging on the other's and without any means of influence on it.

Of course, the president can send messages to Congress and veto its legislation; but the messages have only a moral value, and the veto was seldom used before 1914. Certainly, the Senate can oppose nominations made by the president; but seldom does so, and only in a restricted area. What is essential is that Congress cannot coerce the president by forcing him to resign; the impeachment procedure, which is in itself exceptional, has been invoked only once, and without success. Conversely, the president cannot coerce Congress; he cannot call for a vote of confidence, that weapon so powerful in Europe in forcing the passage of a law or a budget.

Between 1870 and 1914 the American presidential system was much weaker and much less efficient than European parliamentarian government. This weakness of the central government of the United States was accentuated by the lack of a career administrative corps. In the beginning, the spoils system dominated the administration, which meant that after virtually every election the political faithful were rewarded with administrative posts. In 1883, the Pendleton Civil Service Act made the first move toward the replacement of the spoils system by a civil service on the European model, but it covered only slightly more than 10 percent of the federal jobs.

The spoils system was dominant until 1889. It meant mediocre, incompetent, corrupt, unreliable personnel. There was a vast contrast with the European administrations, developed by the kings over the centuries to bolster their power against the feudal lords and then utilized by bourgeois governments to strengthen theirs. It was not only stability, competence, and honesty that were involved, but also a concept of the state that had been developing since the days of the medieval lawyers. At that time, no such notion of the state existed in the United States. One might legitimately say that public opinion was strongly opposed to it; the devotion to free enterprise and the phobia about public intervention in the economy reinforced the basic suspicion and distrust of federal authority.

No theoretician of constitutional law could confuse the American presidential system with European parliamentarianism; but their differences are less visible to the layman. It is not overly important that the chief of state and the chief of government are two separate individuals in Europe, whereas one man holds both posts in the United States. Monarchs have lost almost all their influence on political life and have become national symbols; and, indeed, this brought them new respect and affection, as the case of Victoria showed in Britain. They in no way hampered the prime minister, who has almost as much freedom of action as the president of the United States. The European chief of government's is limited more by the possible weakness or rebellion of his parliamentary majority than by the presence of a virtually paralyzed chief of state at his side.

The most important difference lies in the procedures for selecting the president and the prime minister. The latter is designated by the king and has to win either the parliament's express confidence or its tacit approval. He can be forced to resign by a vote of no confidence by the parliament. The president is chosen by the electoral college, selected in each state according to rules laid down by its legislature. Congress plays no part in his accession to power and cannot remove him, barring exceptional circumstances. The House of Representatives would choose the president and the Senate would select the vice-president, if no candidate could win an absolute majority in the electoral college. This has happened only twice in the history of the United States, in 1800 and 1824.

The framers of the American Constitution preferred not to have the president directly elected by the people and instead decreed that he be chosen by a body of leaders. They wanted the electors to constitute a college of "wise men" competent to select the "best." The procedure did not evolve as they had hoped, because, in the last analysis, the electors turned out to be mere straw men, and the nation came very close to direct universal suffrage. A parallel development led to the same results in the parliamentary systems. Since the nineteenth century, the dualism and discipline of the British parties have made the parliamentary elections more and more like direct popular elections of the chief of government; voting Liberal or Conservative was, in a sense, like voting for Gladstone or Disraeli as prime minister.

The differences are much more fundamental with regard to the relations between the executive and the parliament. As previously noted, in Europe the prime minister may be overthrown by the members of the popularly elected chamber, if they refuse him their vote of confidence.

In the United States, the procedure of impeachment allows the Representatives to accuse the president before the Senate, which may find him guilty by a vote of at least two-thirds of its members. In Europe this power of the parliaments became the source of political responsibility. But in the United States this was not so: the only president impeached, Andrew Johnson, was found innocent. The fact that the president cannot be overthrown by Congress has put him in a different position from that of prime ministers. Yet one must distinguish theory from practice. In the greatest number of parliamentary systems, the legislature rarely overthrew the government between 1870 and 1914 and thus the European systems fairly closely resembled the American system.

Parliaments

The parliaments of continental Europe and the Congress of the United States are the institutions of the Western system patterned after the model of the British Houses of Parliament. In Europe the parliament represents the assertion of democratic power based on elections against hereditary monarchs, who were slowly confined to a symbolic role or even entirely eliminated, as in France. In the New World the first Congress at Philadelphia was the first expression of the nation and its will to be independent. The distinction thus made between legislative and executive power suggests clearly the supremacy of the first and the subordination of the second, an idea which corresponds not only to the formation of plutodemocracies but also to the ideology of liberalism. The state must be as weak as possible, limited to the elementary tasks of keeping internal order and maintaining the national defense, in order not to repress individuals and in particular not to interfere with private economic initiative and competition.

By reducing the executive power to the execution of laws, the only organ capable of intervention in the economy was weakened. When in the 1930's it became necessary to control the private economy, to regulate it and to direct it, the legislature was to yield power to the executive—but that is another story. The respect of the liberals for the parliament and law is not dangerous for the businessman. Although in theory the parliaments had enough weapons to destroy capitalism and establish a collectivist system, in practice such a legal revolution proved impossible during the period 1870-1914. The working-class parties could never get a majority in parliament, and indeed such an idea was almost unthinkable. And even had the working class obtained a majority, the parliaments would have been by their very nature and structure incapable of directing a Socialist economy.

These legislatures were, however, well adapted to the functions of the liberal state: to establish equality of rights among all the citizens in order to protect the initiative of each and the competition of all, to maintain the institution of private property and the principles through which it is acquired, and to determine the nature of contractual relations and provide sanctions for the nonfulfillment of contracts. These legislatures also established the laws concerning marriage, adoption, and inheritance in order to guarantee private property. They assured civil rights and provided for the maintenance of internal order. Even today all of these tasks are better carried out by the legislatures than by executive orders and regulations prepared by the administration. The structure of these legislatures that made it difficult for them to take charge of the economy made them an excellent instrument of legislation in civil and criminal matters. Dealing with these was their major task in the period between 1870 and 1914.

The same qualities are necessary to participate in electoral contests and win the support of the voters: the abilities to raise particular problems to the level of general principles, to express them with the greatest possible clarity, to discuss the possible solutions, and to arrive at a conclusion that takes into account all the interests involved. Such qualities are particularly in evidence among lawyers, judges, professors, writers, and newspapermen, all of whom, in fact, have played a very important role in the legislatures of the liberal state. Their incompetence in economic matters was considered a virtue, since it meant that they constituted no threat to the businessman.

Nonetheless, the style and the level of the debates, the quality and the extent of legislation were very different on the two sides of the Atlantic. In Europe, where the aristocracy continued to retain positions of influence or where conservative ideologies maintained some following, the parliaments persevered in their struggle to establish freedom. They enjoyed prestige, they attracted men of quality, and they confronted the great problems. In the United States, where liberal democracy was not contested, where political conformity was the rule, and where many laws were made by the state legislatures rather than by

Congress, this latter body was not particularly distinguished. Its members were often mediocre and their debates were often rather narrow in scope. Besides the Congress and the executive shared more or less equal powers, and the Supreme Court could set aside any act of Congress on the grounds of unconstitutionality.

In Europe, by contrast, the theory of the supremacy of parliament was developed. This supremacy was achieved not merely because of the historic role that parliament played in the formation of liberal democracy, but also because of the concern for protection against popular pressures. The representative assemblies replaced the people as the spokesmen of national sovereignty. Those who made the French constitution of 1789 wrote into it ideas expressed by Edmund Burke in Great Britain in the form of an extremely important doctrine. According to it the source of political power is not the citizens but the "nation"—an abstract and mysterious entity represented in the legislatures. Thus we move from the sovereignty of the people to the sovereignty of the nation and from the sovereignty of the nation to the sovereignty of the parliament. This ingenious construction glosses over the contradiction between liberal ideology, which finds the source of political power in the people, and the bourgeoisie's determination not to be overwhelmed by the proletariat. This idea spread widely and lawyers in Europe still make use of it. Even in the middle of the twentieth century President Paul Reynaud announced in the National Assembly: "France is here in this very place."

In the United States, where federalism prevented the adoption of the theory of parliamentary sovereignty, the same practical results were reached by less ideological means. The growth of the Congressional committees, their structure and powers, gave the control of Congress to a small number and allowed them to become a bulwark against the vagaries of universal suffrage. This development appears to have been particularly necessary because the franchise was more extended in the United States than in Europe. Electoral landslides could, and still can, be contained by the organization of the legislature, which gives considerable power to the small group of representatives who have been in office the longest. The principle of seniority by which Congress appoints committee members thus gives old men the majority representation in the Congressional committees, through which all bills must be channeled before they come to the floor for a public debate. Furthermore the chairman of a committee is practically irremovable and has large powers at his command. In the House of Representatives a majority of the Rules Committee (appointed by the Speaker of the House in 1910) can prevent any bill from being discussed even after it has been reported by the committee. Thus can Congress be semi-paralyzed.

In Europe parliaments do not go that far. Nowhere are the powers of the parliamentary committees as great as in the United States, nor is the rule of seniority accepted. Yet the system of permanent committees favors the dominance of the older members of parliament and allows for the creation of an older inner circle that controls assemblies in various countries, as in the case of France and Sweden. This is less the case in Great Britain, where the parties in the House of Commons are better organized.

Bicameralism offers another protection against the people. In Europe it was first used to maintain the aristocratic component under pluto-democracy. With the exception of Norway, all European nations have a bicameral system. The "upper" chamber, and the adjective is character-istic, is generally the refuge of the nobility. The clearest example of this is Great Britain's House of Lords, whose members are named for life by the king or hold their seats by hereditary right. Until the Parliament Act of 1911, which greatly diminished the power of the Lords, they had more or less the same powers as members of the House of Com-mons, except in matters of finance, which had first to be examined by the House.

In continental Europe the aristocratic character of the upper chamber is less apparent. In Denmark, the king appoints for life twelve of the sixty-six members of the Landsting. In Holland, the monarch appointed all the members of the upper house until the reform of 1848 that provided their election. In the other countries, the elective principle applied to the selection of the upper chamber, but the electoral laws gave a preponderant position to the aristocracy or to the upper bour-geoisie; first, a system of indirect elections assured that the upper chamber is elected by provincial or municipal electors; and second, until 1914, the franchise for the election of the upper house was more restricted than that for the lower house. In this manner the preponder-ance of the rural interests, which were linked to the aristocracy and to conservative ideologies, was assured. Occasionally a high income was required before one could vote. Thus in 1867 sixty-four of the eighty-two members of the upper chamber in Sweden were rich nobles, and they were a conservative majority in that country for a long time. In Denmark the farmers and the conservative groups controlled the Landsting. In Belgium the majority of the Senate was long composed of the big landowners. In France, the rural groups long had an overwhelming representation in the assemblies. In fact this provision for the French Senate was the condition for the acceptance of the constitution of 1875 by the moderate forces of the aristocracy. One might say that the French Senate was the price that had to be paid to the monarchists for their acceptance of the republic. In 1876, 52 percent of its members were royalists.

The upper chambers of European legislatures evolved with the passage of time. In the beginning a refuge of the nobility, they eventually became a refuge of the bourgeoisie and a bulwark against popular demands; that is, they became strongholds of the economic oligarchy.

In the American Congress bicameralism assumes a different character. It developed through a compromise between the big states, which favored representation on the basis of population, and the small ones, which favored an assembly in which the states were represented equally. This mechanism was later adopted by all the federal systems. But the upper chamber was used, as in Europe, as a breakwater against the tides of democracy. The words of Washington to Jefferson on the role of the United States Senate, which was elected indirectly by the legislatures of the states until 1913, comes to mind. "You pour your coffee in the saucer to cool it off; we pour the bills into the Senatorial saucer to cool them off."

It should be pointed out in conclusion that parliaments are double-edged swords. They are both the expression of popular sovereignty and a means of containing it. They become the means by which the bourgeoisie comes to power; they help maintain it in power by creating a political system that protects it from the people's importunities. They can also dislodge the bourgeoisie from power if suffrage is made truly universal—if inequalities of representation are eliminated—if bicameralism is abolished, and so on. The ambivalence of the role of parliaments explains, perhaps, why the theme of their "decline" appeared at the very time when they begin to play an important role in political life.

The "golden age" of parliaments can be situated in the period 1870-

1914—but many at that time were already speaking of their decline. Does not this hide perhaps an unconscious hope? The bourgeoisie had every interest in supporting parliaments in the period of aristo-monarchy, which they helped destroy, and during the first stages of liberal democracy, when they gave the bourgeoisie protection. But the same bourgeoisie began to turn against parliaments when it realized that, as the instruments of universal suffrage, they might be used by the people to challenge the domination of the bourgeoisie.

Political Parties

In accordance with the individualism of liberal democracy, political parties usually had weak structures that left a great deal of liberty to their members. Until 1914, it was forbidden in some countries to allude to parties in the parliament. There were only deputies, who were sepa-rated from one another and, in theory, independent.

At the end of the nineteenth century, however, socialist parties began to organize; their deputies were subject to the authority of an executive committee that imposed strict discipline. They made no substantial change in the structure of liberal democracy before 1914, for they were always in the opposition, though prepared at times to support a minis-try with their votes. Circumstances changed between 1918 and 1939, when they entered the government in many European countries (Brit-ain, Weimar Germany, Scandinavia, Belgium, France, and so on). Large mass organizations also emerged on the right and in the center—Fascist and certain Christian Democratic parties. These developments occurred in the intermediate period between liberal democracy and the con-temporary Western system of technodemocracy.

European Parties

The word *party* antedated liberal democracy. In earlier systems, it meant a clan established around important personalities, such as power-ful barons, esteemed courtiers, princes of the blood. True parties, in the modern sense of the word, came into being with parliaments and elec-tions, the functioning of which they made possible. They appeared, at first, in the form of parliamentary groups. Now and again in the assem-blies of estates, coalitions would be formed that would cut across the division of "orders"; the minor clergy making common cause with the peasants and the middle class, some members of the upper middle class drawing closer to the upper nobility, and so on. These combinations were usually short-lived. In the British House of Commons, the permanence of the institution led to the permanence of groups. But although parliamentary groups were the first forms of political parties, they were not particularly cohesive. The first genuine manifestation of political parties were the "electoral committees" formed in each district to sponsor candidates. Influential personages, well known and respected, met to choose those who would seek the citizens' votes, to stand moral surety for them in a sense, to attest to their good character and their ability to represent the district properly, and to organize the campaign, particularly through the solicitation of the money required. The committees thus set up tended to survive after the election in order to make sure that the winners would keep their pledges or, in the case of losers, to plan for revenge. They played an important part in the political process. Their members were the real political authorities in the district.

Naturally, those election committees that shared similar views were led to unite in national organizations. When one of these was formed, it was a true party, in the modern meaning of the word. As a rule, these were not highly centralized organizations, and the local committees retained much of their independence. Their delegates met in congresses to name a central committee. In the British parties, this was more likely to be tantamount to the parliamentary group, which had a stronger structure than any other, probably as a result of its long experience; the leader of each party was named by its parliamentary group after his predecessor's death or retirement.

The term *leader parties*, which I applied to organizations of this kind in 1951, has been generally adopted. Such a party makes no appeal to the popular masses, nor does it develop a system of formal membership as the socialists were to do at the end of the nineteenth century. Each local committee consists only of important figures whose influence matters more than their number. These notables always include a businessman or someone trusted by businessmen, who finance election campaigns and the party organization in general. National leadership is actually exercised by known political leaders around whom cliques take shape, not dissimilar to those that formed in the past around influential aristocrats capable of enjoying the confidence of the throne. Behind or alongside them are prominent members of the economic oligarchy.

The first parties were established by the middle class. To replace a system based on the nobility, the middle class set up one founded on leaders, so that it could simultaneously dislodge the aristocracy and bring the masses into line. As a rule, then, liberal parties appeared before conservative parties. For a long time, they remained better organized and more doctrinaire. When one seeks to replace an established order with a new system, one has to be able to present a relatively precise picture of it. Ideology is more necessary to the left than to the right, which can confine itself to the defense of existing structures in empiric fashion, without proposing anything new. On the other hand, elections without organized parties afforded an advantage to those who, for centuries, had been the best known and the most revered, the nobles. Any middle-class personality taken singly carried less weight; only the coalition of all of them in a committee offered them sufficient power of attraction.

The electoral and parliamentary effectiveness of parties was to drive the aristocracy to create one of its own. To better justify the established order, it would have to construct an ideology, too. Thus, conservative organizations began to grow, modeled on their liberal predecessors. These were essentially the two major adversaries until the end of the nineteenth century. Plutodemocracy arose through their conflicts, which were essentially class struggles, with the reservations that have been stated earlier. The liberal parties represented the interests of the industrial and mercantile class; they tended to entrust power to bankers, businessmen, and industrialists, as they withdrew it from princes, dukes, marquesses, counts, and other hereditary aristocrats, who gave battle by means of their conservative parties.

The liberals were backed by urban wage-earners, not to mention artisans and small shopkeepers; the conservatives were supported by the peasants. For a long time, then, the conservative-liberal conflict was simultaneously a struggle between the aristocracy and the middle class and between city and country. Some country dwellers, however, supported the liberals, who could not have triumphed unaided in a world in which the agricultural population was by far the largest. In Britain, the alliance between the middle class and the county aristocracy went back very far and seemed to have played a decisive part in the evolution of Parliament. In Scandinavia, a liberal agrarian party emerged parallel to the urban liberal party, providing for the separate representation of the peasantry and the urban middle class in national legislatures of the region. The conflict was three- rather than two-sided.

In other countries, this pattern was complicated by the super-imposition of other conflicts on the basic clash between liberals and conservatives. In the Netherlands, the conservatives were divided into two groups, Catholic and Protestant, and then into three, when there was a schism among the Protestants; the "historical Christians" opposed the "antirevolutionaries." In France, each of the two major tendencies was divided between moderates and extremists, who could not live together in the same parties. Hence, there were "Jacobins" and "Re-publicans" alongside the moderate liberals, and "Orléanists" alongside the "legitimists," or ultraconservatives. Conflicts over the nature of the political regime brought further complications; the moderate liberals and conservatives were split among those who favored parliamentary monarchy, those who backed a republic, and those who wanted Bona-partism.

These variations do not alter the general scheme of parties. Before 1870, in general, the conflict was fierce and implacable, except in Brit-ain; conservatives wanted to preserve the aristo-monarchy, and liberals sought to establish plutodemocracy. The conservatives usually enlisted religion as their ally, especially in the Catholic parties, and this thrust liberalism toward anticlericalism. By the end of the century, the ques-tion was an anachronism, though many refused to acknowledge the fact. The decline of the old order was obvious and general, and the accession of liberal democracy had become inevitable. Little by little, the conservatives resigned themselves to it, except for the sentimental and the intransigent. The gap between the two parties became nar-rower, and the class conflict between aristocracy and bourgeoisie faded out.

This reconciliation was encouraged by the emergence and growth of Socialist parties. The former enemies were forced to fraternize to de-fend a basic (one might almost say "a capital") common interest—private property. Thus began the transition from the great conflict of the nineteenth century—conservative against liberal—to that of the twentieth—capitalist against Socialist. The trend was clear even before 1914. It ripened between the wars. In a number of countries it was to culminate in a merger of the old liberal and conservative parties in a broad organization opposed to the Socialists. But this point was not reached until the time of the Second World War—that is, in the second phase of plutodemocracy, which will be examined presently.

The evolution of Socialist parties had another effect on conservative and liberal organizations. It forced them to modify their structures and seek the participation of the masses. The need for this had already become apparent in the closing years of the nineteenth century, when the structure of the leader parties was becoming too narrow in relation to the extension of the right to vote and the desire of a large number of persons to take an active part in politics. In the United States this took the form of the demand for "primaries." In Britain, Disraeli made a remarkable experiment in 1883 with the Primrose League, which gave the Conservative party an auxiliary organization that was open to new members. Liberal committees proliferated, opening their ranks to the "new classes" of society—the petite bourgeoisie and the workers.

The leader parties, however, continued, until 1914, to be the essential bases for the functioning of liberal democracy. It was only after 1918 that they had to confront the growing opposition of the mass parties and occasionally to share power with them. With these few exceptions, plutodemocracy depended on a few tens of thousands of notables who chose election candidates, financed campaigns, and kept the deputies in line. These notables were not chosen by election; they chose themselves and co-opted others. They were closely connected with businessmen and economic oligarchs, who sometimes themselves were members of party committees, or were represented in them by men beholden to them. These leaders, however, maintained contact with the voters, whose final approval at the polls was necessary. Thus, the leader parties represented a link between formal democratic institutions and the economic oligarchy.

American Parties

Political parties in the United States performed the same function of linking the official democratic structures with the oligarchy that in fact ran the state. Consequently, they adopted a structure similar to that of the European liberals and conservatives, with certain differences that will be discussed later. They did not appeal to the masses; they consisted of prominent persons; they were decentralized; they imposed no voting discipline on members of Congress. A few thousand politicians in each organization acted as transmission belts through which businessmen and the managers of the economy ran the political institutions and sought the support of the voters. But there was a fundamental difference. The American parties did not represent social classes, as the European conservatives and liberals did. As I have previously noted, the United States had no true aristocrats.

Because they had no such definite social base, the American parties encountered much greater difficulty than the Europeans in their development, although the extension of election to a large number of offices and the necessity of organizing presidential elections made the existence of political organizations more necessary and more urgent. Until the great crisis of 1861-1865, the parties in the United States were rather indistinguishable. They had little structure, little stability, little differentiation one from another. In the early years of the United States, two groups came into being, Federalists and Anti-Federalists. Jefferson's election of 1800 confirmed the extinction of the former and the transformation of the latter into the "Democratic Republican party," which was relatively organized. For almost thirty years, this dominant group was opposed only by disparate factions that took a long time to collaborate. They succeeded in 1832, when they assured Andrew Jackson's crushing victory. His supporters, the "Whigs," revived a two-party climate in opposition to the Democratic Republicans, who gradually came to be known simply as Democrats.

In the 1850's, the question of slavery became the major issue in political clashes. Thus, elements drawn from the Whigs, the northern Democrats, and other groups came together in a new party advocating the legal equality of blacks and whites, the Republican party, which scored successes in 1856 and elected Abraham Lincoln to the presidency in 1860. Thereafter, the old Democratic party was disorganized and weakened by the war; it lost its northern backers because of its ties with the South but—gradually, it recovered them. After the compromise of 1877, it succeeded in creating an alliance between the interests of the South and those of the northern workers and farmers, an alliance that placed it in a strong position.

Nevertheless, the Republican party retained the place of dominance until the election of Franklin D. Roosevelt. In the seventy-two years between 1861 and 1933, the Democrats occupied the White House for only sixteen years, from 1881 to 1885 and from 1889 to 1893 under Grover Cleveland, and from 1913 to 1921 under Woodrow Wilson. The party of the new immigrants, the tenant farmers, the workers, the Catholics, and the South, the Democratic party was the umbrella for disparate minorities—including the black voters in the northern cities. The "old" Republican party was the embodiment of traditional, Anglo-Saxon, Protestant America, above all of the America of industry and businessmen. The Republicans' long tenure had no equivalent in Europe during the same period. It attested to the dominance of the industrial middle class, which was opposed by no other deeply rooted class—such as the aristocracy in the Old World—but only by numerous conflicting groups.

The rivalry between the American parties was to a large degree not ideological. It had to do with concrete problems, usually limited—customs tariffs, bimetalism, and so forth—since both parties had adopted the liberal ideology. But political conflicts did acquire an ideological aspect about the middle of the nineteenth century. The great debate on slavery transcended the practical problems raised by the use of slave labor and the rights of blacks. It was concerned with an issue of principle that went to the very concept of man and society. This departure from habit had no happy consequence, for it ended in a bloody civil war.

While the American parties were leader parties, like the European liberals and conservatives of the same period, the differences in structure are important. In the United States, party organization is weaker at the top and stronger at the base. The national party is only a very weak confederation of the parties in all the states. President Eisenhower's statement in 1956 was even more valid in the nineteenth century and at the beginning of the twentieth: "There are no national parties in the United States. There are forty-eight state parties, and consequently they decide who belongs to them: I have no right to state that any one of them is not Republican."

The strong development of local party organization results, first of all, from the importance of the local electoral task, which is much greater in the United States than in Europe. Federalism makes it necessary for the voter to elect not only the president, the Senators, and the Representatives but also the governor, the members of the state legislature, and the local officials. Moreover, many lower posts are elective, while in Europe their occupants would be designated by political and administrative authorities: sheriffs, judges, prosecutors, comptrollers, and so forth. The number of elective posts in the United States today is reckoned at seven hundred thousand. It was much smaller in the nineteenth and early twentieth centuries, but it was still very high in comparison with the situation in Europe. The parties nominated the candidates for each of these posts. This was a very important and very complicated business that required a highly developed organization.

On the other hand, the parties were equally important in the selection of appointive officeholders: positions were doled out to the supporters of the victorious party and redistributed whenever a majority was overthrown. However weak the liberal American state, however undeveloped its public administration, there were always plenty of spoils to be shared. Furthermore, certain local positions, the salaries for which were paid by the municipality or the state, were reserved to party "career men," thus strengthening the organization.

Hence, the American parties played a much greater part in the normal institutional structure of the United States than did the European parties in their countries. At times, they went outside this structure to set up powerful "machines" on the local and regional levels that had varying effects on the functioning of democracy. In view of the fact that in a town the police commissioner, the prosecutor, the judge, the head of the fiscal administration, and so forth, were elected by the citizens, a party that succeeded in having its candidates elected to these posts, as well as the town council and the mayor's office, would control the entire city. If the party was run by a dynamic, unscrupulous boss, he could become an autocrat and, through violence and corruption, keep a firm grip on the power thus acquired.

The "machines" were merely the hypertrophy of the normal organization of American parties. The number of elective posts to be filled and the quantity of spoils to be distributed, the parochialism of political activity, the belief in what worked, the need for a boss—all these things naturally operated together to invest local party leaders with great power. In a period of economic expansion based on ruthless competition and fanatic quest for profit, a certain lack of scruple was unavoidable. It was not easy to draw the line between the "political boss" and the gangster. Few local party organizations were completely honest, few were completely dishonest—the pendulum oscillated to and fro above a median line, with some violent lunges in one direction, as in the Prohibition era.

At the end of the nineteenth century, the excesses of these party organizations aroused the anger of many Americans, who exerted all their efforts to put an end to them. This was the origin of the campaign for primary elections, the aim of which was to establish the nomination of candidates through popular election rather than selection by party organs. It led to major electoral reforms in the early twentieth century; these cut slightly, but only slightly, into the powers of the party machines. Instead of offering a single party candidate, the organization now proposed several, among whom the voters chose in the primary. Except in so-called nonpartisan primaries—which were rare—candidates who were independent of the organizations had little hope of being nominated by the voters.

This power wielded by the party apparatus, regardless of whether it attained the proportions of a "machine," did not necessarily have harmful effects. American political parties performed a certain social function with respect to the immigrants who were pouring in from Europe in great waves. Lost in a world that was totally new to him, the stranger found no public agency set up to help and guide him. Economic liberalism was superbly unconcerned with his fate. All that mattered was his capacity to work, which must be harnessed as soon as possible without unnecessary expenditures. Each man's ingenuity was supposed to make it possible for him to find the place to which he was best suited. Providing for the immigrants would have interfered with capitalist competition, and nothing could have been more injurious.

But to the parties, the immigrants represented potential votes. To help them find housing and work and a place in a community of their compatriots, in exchange for the promise of their votes in the future, was a profitable undertaking in which many political organizations engaged, especially on the east coast. It is easy to understand Walter Lippmann's barbed doubt whether the city of New York could be "as human, as kind and as gay as Tammany Hall." European immigrants were not the only beneficiaries of this solicitude; it was available to all the unfortunate who needed help in exchange for their votes. In Atlantic City, a party organization man named Nocky Johnson kept a yard full of coal for poor blacks, who could always fill their bags with it for nothing. An organization man in Boston said: "I consider it essential that every neighborhood should have someone to whom any poor devil can turn for help." The price of this social service was usually high for the community as a whole. But it filled a basic need that was otherwise left unsatisfied.

The two major parties established in the United States about the time of the Civil War, the Republicans and the Democrats, had no serious rivals before 1939—or after. This was in dramatic contrast to Europe, where large Socialist parties emerged at the end of the nineteenth century. We shall examine later the factors that were hostile to a similar evolution in the United States. The "Populist" surge in the 1890's, however, was much stronger than that of any other third party, none of which was of any importance in American political life. Some scholars believe the Populists might have been able to challenge the established parties. Their rise seems to have corresponded to the resentment that farmers and the lower middle class felt against the domination of businessmen. At the same time, Europe was experiencing the upsurge of the "new classes"; this was not a Socialist movement but a spasm within liberal capitalism that tended, though without success, toward the redistribution of power within the economic oligarchy.

Chapter Five
The Economic Oligarchy

On the surface, liberal democracy gives the impression of profound unity. The political structure and the economic structure seem to rest on the same foundations: equality, freedom, pluralism, competition, and representation. The equality of the right to vote and to run for office is paralleled by the equality of the right to choose one's profession, to found a company, and to direct it to one's liking. The freedom of expression has for a corollary the freedom of industrial invention. The competition of political parties during elections is equivalent to the rivalry of firms in the market. The representative assemblies—municipal, regional, and national—correspond to the shareholders' meetings of commercial companies. The political executive—elected directly or indirectly—can be compared with chairmen of the board designated under the same conditions. Political liberalism and economic liberalism seem to be cut from the same cloth.

The reality is quite different, because private ownership of the means of production, the basis of every economy, introduces an element of inequality that is perpetuated by inheritance. Let us imagine a group of men disembarking in a new land, all possessing the same capital at the outset and equitably dividing the soil, idealized Pilgrims of the *Mayflower* in a sense. In accordance with the differences in their physical strength, intelligence, astuteness, health, work, and luck, they will progressively cease to be equal. At their death, some will possess rather extensive assets—in arable land, tools, machines, workshops, warehouses; others, more modest assets; others, no capital. Equality no longer exists at the outset of the second generation, some having greater possibilities for action than others. Undoubtedly, certain inefficient sons will squander their fathers' capital, while others, born without capital, will learn how to acquire it. It is true, nevertheless, that the original capitalists have many more advantages in competition and that these advantages grow from generation to generation.

Thus, a fundamental contradiction developed in the liberal democracies. They established political equality by suppressing the privileges of the aristocracy. But they progressively developed economic inequality, which tended to recreate a new aristocracy, founded on capitalistic ownership. The inheritance of fortunes succeeded the inheritance of titles of nobility; the heredity of economic power supplanted the heredity of political power. Alexis de Tocqueville saw in the United States the advent of "a manufacturing aristocracy . . . one of the toughest that had appeared on the earth." During the same period, Stendhal was of the opinion that in France "the bank is the head of state: the bourgeoisie has replaced the Faubourg Saint-Germain and the bank is the nobility of the middle class." Thus economic democracy was very soon replaced by feudal relations of a new kind. And the weakness of the political system encouraged the emergence and power of the new aristocracy—there was no king to oppose the new barons of finance, industry, and trade that came to dominate the state.

At the end of the nineteenth century the domination of these new barons came up against the growing opposition of the middle classes. Small entrepreneurs fought against the concentration of firms. The American progressive movement and European radicalism were expressions of the growth of these new groups. But since these new classes did not represent any challenge to the capitalist order, they could not seriously threaten the powers of the oligarchy, which was willing to make certain concessions; for instance, it acceded to the income tax, but it took every precaution to limit the effects of the levy. Or it would divert the demands of the middle classes into areas that held no menace for large companies, the prohibition of alcohol in the United States, or anticlericalism in Catholic Europe. Nationalism and colonial imperialism played important parts in this connection. They benefited the economic interests of the upper middle class while, at the same time, affording psychological satisfactions to the lower middle class. In France, protectionist customs duties and high agricultural prices augmented the profits of the oligarchy and, at the same time, made it possible for production by obsolete methods to survive. Everywhere progressivism and radicalism were "integrated" without too much difficulty, and discrepancies within capitalism were coped with. The lords

71

of the economy would have to reckon with the minor nobility, the ladies-in-waiting and the baronets, but without any real disturbance of their own dominance. The economic oligarchy did not cease to rule or to be an oligarchy; its power was simply rendered less absolute, and it had to become somewhat more sensitive to the demands of the middle classes and the wage-earners.

The Instruments of Oligarchic Power

The economic oligarchy did not constitute a coherent and organized group, but a conglomeration of individuals and groups opposed to each other. This fact leads many liberal authors to conclude that it could not exercise leadership and control. They speak of "social pluralism" as the basis of democracy. Nobody can contest the existence of such a pluralism nor can one question the existence of competition between various groups and within groups; each man was lord of his enterprise and rivaled his counterpart. But the rivalries of firms did not destroy the solidarity of the businessmen any more than rivalry had undermined the solidarity of the lords in the aristo-monarchical period. Both classes united against external dangers. In fact, profit was a more potent unifying force for the bourgeoisie than "blood" was for the nobility. There were cases in which noblemen united with the peasants in order to destroy another nobleman: there is no such case among the members of the bourgeoisie in times of a social revolution. All the entrepreneurs spontaneously united against the demands of the workers and state controls. In short, social pluralism was superficial and existed only within the economic oligarchy. All its members were welded together by a deep belief in the efficacy of free enterprise and its moral supremacy and by the fear of the popular pressures that universal suffrage and democratic institutions encourage. The whole constituted a powerful bloc that dominated the state as it dominated production.

Nonetheless this domination was not absolute. *The Communist Manifesto* stated that "modern government is merely a delegation that manages the common business of the entire middle class." The description was quite adequate for the state of affairs in 1848. It became an exaggeration with the growth of liberal democracy, as popular pressure made itself felt through political parties, labor unions, trade associations, and so on. Government was no longer solely a delegation of the middle class, though to a large extent it was still this. The term "delegation" is very apt: the economic oligarchy hardly controlled politics in a direct fashion. In Europe, for a short period, bankers and businessmen assumed the principal parliamentary and ministerial positions, but that situation quickly became the exception. In the United States capitalists took part in the management of the state for a longer time and to a greater degree. The businessmen of the north gradually replaced the planters of Virginia in Congress and in the government.

The "Intermediate Class"

The oligarchy controlled the economy directly but managed politics indirectly, through a kind of "intermediate class" made up of politicians, civil servants, and the manipulators of public opinion. The first comprised, basically, the holders of governmental offices, ministers, deputies, senators, governors, mayors, members of regional and local legislatures, and so forth. These official personages constituted the centers round which the professional staffs and active workers of the political parties revolved, assuring direct communication between the elected officials and the citizens who elected them. The American parties and the European liberal and conservative parties constituted a fundamental basis for the intermediate class before 1914. At this time, however, the Socialist parties were making every effort to prevent the domination of politics by the economic oligarchy. Between the two world wars, they were, little by little, assimilated into liberal democracy, and at the same time, they became more receptive to the influence of the oligarchy; they, too, in part, became in fact an element of the intermediate class.

Public employees represented another category in this class. In the United States, they could hardly be distinguished, at that time, from the politicians, since the spoils system made it possible for these to distribute jobs as they pleased by way of reward to their supporters. Often the parties' staff workers were taken care of in this way. The same technique existed in Europe at the local level—in the provinces, large regions, and, in particular, towns. The situation at the national level was different; the British Civil Service, the German administration, the large French public services constituted entities with strong traditions, permanence of tenure, and a recruiting system based more or less on competitive examination. But, in spite of these provisions, their autonomy was limited.

The third category of the intermediate class was made up of all those who had a hand in the shaping of public opinion, teachers at all levels, educational administrators, journalists, writers, intellectuals, priests and pastors, and so on. In theory, liberal democracy did not promulgate any specific ideological doctrine; it tended simply to develop common sense, reason, and the critical mind, which would enable each man to judge for himself. In practice, the citizens of the West have been conditioned from childhood through the school, the church, and family custom to respect certain basic principles, notably, private property, free enterprise, competition, profit-seeking, all of which predispose them to respect the economic oligarchy and to accept its influence. An analysis of school textbooks, works for religious instruction, popular newspapers, and books on best-seller lists would demonstrate that they tend to foster such a conformity.

The economic oligarchy dominated the intermediate classes by means of various techniques. Financial pressure played an important part. Many teachers, at various levels, and journalists were directly or indirectly being paid by the heads of companies. The public employees dependent on the spoils system, the party cadres, and the staffs of the schools, the universities, and the churches subsidized by businessmen were indirectly their employees, in a certain sense. Individual corruption, too, was widespread among politicians. In the United States, if John Kenneth Galbraith is to be believed, "in the heroic days of individual ownership . . . it was assumed that congressmen and senators would be the spokesmen, paid or otherwise, of the industrial firms of their states or districts. From those so financed or controlled, the entrepreneurial corporation got much of what it wanted. The control was not absolute but it was sufficiently extensive to justify belief in corporate domination of the state as a normal fact of life."[1] The thing was managed more discreetly in Europe, where it was less openly accepted by the public, though it was scarcely less prevalent.

More subtle forms of financial pressure reinforced these elementary

1. John Kenneth Galbraith, *The New Industrial State,* 2nd ed. rev. (Boston: Houghton Mifflin, 1971), p. 301.

techniques. The politics of social relations with high public officials, as developed by French businessmen, afforded a good example of this kind of financial pressure. The businessmen attracted the officials to their enterprises by offering high positions to men in the great state administrations, for whom this "going to pasture" (as it was called in the circles where it was practiced) represented great financial advancement. The election of politicans to boards of directors had the same effect. In addition, the economic oligarchy often employed with respect to this intermediate class the same politics of marriage that the traditional aristocracy had used with regard to the wealthy upper middle class a century or two earlier.

Collective pressure was probably stronger still than these private pressures. A politician, a political party, a newspaper, a school, a university, a church that put up too much resistance to the businessman would be deprived of the funds necessary for its activity and would be all but paralyzed unless it succeeded in organizing a system of financing that was totally independent of capitalism. In a material sense, some organizations—such as the labor unions, the political parties, and the newspapers—could manage to do this. But this forced them into a position outside the liberal ideology, for which the profit motive, the growth of private firms, and their freedom of movement represented the essential motivation for growth. Very few were disposed to do this.

Ultimately, liberal ideology proved to be the most effective means of assuring the domination of the economic oligarchy over the intermediate class, because it persuaded that class to accept its position of subordination. To the majority of politicians, civil servants, and shapers of public opinion between 1870 and 1914, private property was "sacred," in the words of the Declaration of the Rights of Man and the Citizen of 1789. Those who saw to its exaltation and assured the most effective material growth of society had somewhat the same character. The harmony between their private and public interests led naturally to a deferential attitude toward businessmen.

None of the members of the intermediate class, however, had ever been totally submissive to the economic oligarchy. Politicians had to be elected and reelected to exercise power; the oligarchs could not impose any candidate they pleased on the voters, nor could they easily get rid of popular political figures. The British Civil Service and the major administrative services in France endowed their members with certain means of resisting the pressures of businessmen, who then denounced "technocracy." The universities and the churches put professors, administrators, and clerics into an analogous position. Large newspapers could acquire the same institutional quality, which to a degree protected the members of their staffs against the owners of big businesses. The domination of the intermediate class by the economic oligarchy was still a far cry from the simplistic concept of "pulling strings." Politicians, civil servants, and shapers of opinion were not mere puppets in the hands of businessmen. Like Petrushka, they could to some extent free themselves from their masters—but only to some extent.

The resistance of the intermediate class to the domination of the economic oligarchy varied greatly from country to country, and the difference was greatest between the United States and the European nations. This resulted in part from the differences in institutions. American federalism and localism played a very important part; the distribution of political power between the states and the cities weakened it considerably in relation to an economic power that was becoming more highly concentrated, and more quickly, than in Europe. Few governors and legislatures were in a position to resist the pressures of businessmen, who were generally much more powerful than they. The lack of a legal code of public service and the persistence of the spoils system contributed to the same result by depriving the United States of a corps of administrators endowed with a sense of public service.

The structure of the political parties accentuates the differences between the United States and Europe with regard to the ability of the intermediate class to resist the oligarchy. On both sides of the Atlantic, the weak, exiguously structured parties with skeleton staffs, composed of politicians rather than citizens capable of withstanding outside pressures, could scarcely put up any effective resistance to the economic oligarchy. In Europe, however, the conservatives contributed to the maintenance of an opposition to the power of money and helped in the defense of altruistic values, in contrast to the domination of the businessman. Against them the liberals had to carry on a difficult struggle for freedom and equality, which led them to insist on the political aspect of their ideology while leaving its capitalistic aspect to one side.

In the United States the situation was different, except during the impassioned time of the Civil War. The lack of any class conflict that challenged the structure of the system of government, and the fact that the political objectives of the liberals had been attained as far back as 1787 through the proclamation of a republic founded on civil equality, political liberty, and national sovereignty, deprived the political parties of an ideological foundation. Thus, they devoted themselves to promoting capitalism. They had not the least intention of resisting the pressures of the economic oligarchy. On the contrary, the dominance of the Republican party was in fact that of the rulers of industry. "If it can be said that the Republican Party has a center of gravity, this center is the same today as it has been since the 1860's—the community of businessmen, of those who direct, advise, supervise and finance American industry and sell its products," the late Clinton Rossiter justly observed;[2] and he cannot be suspected of leftist or Marxist leanings.

Pressure Groups

Nowhere did the economic oligarchy have a central organization that directed and controlled the government. But most branches of the economic oligarchy did develop official organizations in order to promote their own interests, to reinforce their intervention in political life, and to strengthen its domination of the intermediate class. In short, they developed pressure groups. This practice was later adopted by other social groups—the workers, the employees, the veterans, the small farmers, the students—some of which used it very effectively, notably the trade unions.

These pressure groups, especially those in key areas, such as banking, coal, and steel, came to have tremendous power. There were two ways in which these groups completed the economic oligarchy's domination of the intermediate class, which nominally controlled politics. On the one hand, they fortified the authority of the oligarchy's control, as a result of coalition, coordination, and organization. On the other, they made possible a direct influence on public opinion, to which politicians were subject through elections; in this respect they constituted a means of "taking over" the masses of the people by fostering a favorable point of view among them. In this second function, an important part was

2. See Clinton Rossiter, *Parties and Politics in America* (Ithaca: Cornell University Press, 1960).

played by groups that were established without the participation of the economic oligarchy but that upheld its general orientation.

At first such was the case with religious and charitable associations, which multiplied rapidly in the liberal countries. To all appearances, their goals were disinterested: to perfect the morality of their members, to develop love for one's fellow man, and so on. But they accepted the established order implicitly, if not explicitly, and they tended to consolidate it. "Render unto Caesar that which is Caesar's" resulted in justifying Caesar and the capitalism of which he was the incarnation. It will be seen presently that Western religions went to some lengths in this justification, notably by directing their fundamental morality in a certain way. Other groups, ostensibly equally remote from the economic oligarchy, acted similarly in its interests. Veterans' associations fostered the development of nationalism, which tended to conceal the class struggle behind the solidarity of citizenship in a single country. Many youth organizations served to "depoliticize" the new generations and to divert them from real problems. The temperance and morality leagues played the same part for the older generations.

For groups of this type, the principal course of action did not consist of exerting any definite pressure in favor of a concrete reform. It consisted rather of diverting attention of the people to prevent them from recognizing their exploited condition. If they gave their attention to eternal life, their native land, sports, scouting, and the prohibition of alcohol, they would think less about the fact that the product of their labor seemed to enrich their employers. Thus, many groups operating in highly diverse areas had the effect of reinforcing the authority of the economic oligarchy. It did not much matter whether the economic oligarchy had created them on its own initiative, whether it consciously encouraged them, or whether their action was independent.

Not all the pressure groups, however, were the auxiliaries of the oligarchy. Even those that were its tools were not always so. Distracting the people's attention from capitalist exploitation was not the sole purpose of the religious, patriotic, sports, and other organizations. They also expressed independent and natural needs, which might at times be contrary to the interests of the economic oligarchy; then they tended to weaken its authority rather than to reinforce it. In the Third World today, one can observe religious and nationalistic organizations helping in the struggle against neocolonialism. One finds somewhat analogous—

though more marginal—situations in the liberal democracies between 1870 and 1914.

Among the pressure groups that the economic oligarchy itself instituted, many did not express the whole range of its interests but, on the contrary, represented those of a particular group more or less opposed to others, small merchants against large corporations, manufacturers of one product against manufacturers of another, growers of one crop against growers of a different one. The proliferation of local and regional groups in another instance of these "sector" rivalries within the oligarchy. Such rivalries remained limited, because all these special organizations had one common interest to defend: private property and capitalism. The predominant position of businessmen allowed them to control the situation in the last analysis. Some well-organized sectors, however, suceeded in defending themselves effectively; their pressure groups then became "safe houses" and enabled them to preserve particular privileges.

Certain pressure groups, too, were actually opposition organizations, which tended to place direct restraint on the dominance of the oligarchy. Such, at first, was the case of certain citizen organizations that were found in profusion in the United States, in accordance with a process that had already impressed Tocqueville, who wrote in *Democracy in America:* "Americans of all ages, all circumstances and all persuasions unite unceasingly. Not only do they have commercial and industrial associations in which all take part, but they have moreover a thousand other kinds: religious, moral, frivolous, very general and very specific, very large and very small; Americans get together in order to give parties, establish seminaries, build inns, erect churches, distribute books and send missionaries to the Antipodes; in this fashion they set up hospitals, prisons and schools. Finally, if there is a question of bringing a truth to light or of developing an opinion with the support of a great example, they call a meeting."

Most of these groups were local organizations whose influence seldom extended beyond their town lines. They did not seriously challenge the economic oligarchy. Moreover, many supported it directly or indirectly, by defending free enterprise, public morality, and the established order. At the end of the nineteenth century, however, some very strong opposition groups developed on both sides of the Atlantic, the labor unions. In Europe, their appearance and their growth took place within a more general movement, the birth and burgeoning of socialism. In Britain, in Scandinavia, in Belgium, and in Germany, the labor unions formed quite close ties with the Socialist parties and with other unions, such as credit unions, cooperatives, and so on. The whole movement constituted a powerful organization that could counterbalance the economic oligarchy to a certain extent.

In the United States, the development of the unions took a different course. They played little part in politics, particularly in socialism, which barely succeeded in getting a toehold. Like everyone else, they adhered to the liberal ideology and accepted the framework of capitalism, which seemed to them to be the best. Their members thought that a powerful, disciplined organization was necessary to discuss wages and working conditions with the employers; but they had no intention of transforming a society that in their eyes was legitimate. The American labor unions were made an integral part of liberal democracy and introduced practices favorable to wage-earners, especially control of hiring. Finally, they contributed to the evolution of a general consensus in favor of capitalism, and this reinforced the economic oligarchy in its domination.

The Oligarchy and the Masses

In spite of appearances, then, liberal democracy is governed by an oligarchy, as was the aristocratic monarchy that it replaced. But the relations between this oligarchy and the popular masses are radically different; this is the fundamental distinction between the two systems. In the old order, the people were an object, not a subject, of politics; they obeyed the decisions of the rulers without having participated in them; they had no means of influencing them other than agitation in the streets and open rebellion. In a liberal democracy, the people are composed of citizens whose collective sovereignty is acknowledged by the official system of values—that is, the right to adopt drastic measures as a last resort. By means of elections, they designate the rulers, who are named only on a provisional basis and whose mandate to govern must be renewed at regular intervals. The economic oligarchy, based on property and its transfer by inheritance, can control the state only if the popular masses allow it to act. How can it obtain their consent? That is the problem that is to be examined now.

In the official liberal ideology, the problem does not exist. The economic oligarchy is only an illusion. Everyone can become part of it by means of his work and his intelligence, in a system founded on free enterprise and competition. Businessmen have authority only over industry, commerce, and banking, not over politics, in which free elections and the multiparty system guarantee a genuine choice of rulers by the citizens. These rulers are independent, except for taking into account the desires of the voters, who put them into power and can remove them from it. To the Marxists, on the contrary, electoral and parliamentary procedures are illusory; they remain purely formal. Citizens and representatives are totally manipulated by the economic oligarchy. Its wealth allows it to buy consciences and to spread corruption. Above all, it alone possesses the machinery of propaganda, information, and instruction, which shape the beliefs and the votes of the citizens. The oligarchy is real, and it exercises a guiding function in the political realm. But the intervention of the voters is not purely illusory; in spite of all the manipulations that they undergo, they preserve a modicum of autonomy.

Whether this margin is wide, narrow, or nonexistent, there remains the problem of determining how the ruling oligarchy bends the citizens to its will. In this respect, two types of means are conceivable, and both are employed—means of coercion and means of persuasion. The pressure of the popular masses can be contained by force, and they can be broken in this way to subjection by the heads of industry. They can also be persuaded to vote in a given way, and their genuine consent can be obtained. The two methods are sometimes confused. Propaganda can lead to the "statutory rape of the crowd"; the masses conditioned by it have the illusion that they are acting freely, when in reality they are being subjected to irresistible pressure.

The Oligarchy's Defenses against the Masses

In Europe, the middle classes have always been afraid of the popular masses. Liberal ideology has been split by fundamental contradiction between its principle of popular sovereignty, which led to universal suffrage, and the fear in the ruling oligarchy that universal suffrage might lead to the subversion of the social order. As Thiers put it in 1871, "True republicans fear the multitude, the vile multitude that has wrecked all republics." As previously noted, initially this contradiction was overcome by the theory of national sovereignty embodied in the parliament and not in the citizens. In 1791, the French Constituent Assembly took up Burke's ideas on this subject and placed great emphasis on them. Following this example, the nations of Europe went on to establish limited suffrage, based on property or income level, which was to be maintained for a long time, as a rule, until 1914-1918. Before the First World War, only France (since 1848), Germany (since 1871), and Norway (since 1898) had practiced universal suffrage.

In the United States, there was much less mistrust of the people at the outset. Universal suffrage was established in almost all the states at the beginning of the nineteenth century. It extended not only to political institutions but also to administrative, judicial, and police functions. Police chiefs, tax officials, the directors of certain public services, public prosecutors, and judges were generally elected at the same time as city councilors, legislators, governors, members of Congress, and the president of the United States. The mandates were short and the elections were frequent. Nevertheless, the blacks, who were slaves and noncitizens before the Thirteenth Amendment (1865), did not vote; universal suffrage was an illusion in the southern states. After the Civil War, the South had to submit to the federal law that abolished slavery. Many states adopted laws restricting the right to vote by means of property or tax requirements (sometimes making the payment of a special levy, the "poll tax," a prerequisite for voting) or through literacy tests (notably the requirement of ability to explain the Constitution). These provisions were designed to prevent blacks from voting, for the great majority of them were poor and illiterate.

When suffrage became universal, various means were utilized on both sides of the Atlantic to contain the flood of voters. Electoral manipulations were tried. In France, the official candidature practiced by the Second Empire demonstrated the efficacy of the pressure of power. Other examples could be found at the local level. But even at the beginning of the twentieth century, many miners in Carmaux did not dare vote for Jean Jaurès, the Socialist candidate; instead they voted for the Marquis de Solages, lest they risk the loss of their jobs. In rural areas and small towns, the control of the public authorities or the economic oligarchy prevailed for a long time. The artificial designation of electoral districts (gerrymandering) was not without effect either. Out-and-out faking of ballots was rarer, except in certain backward rural regions or in American cities dominated by all-powerful "machines."

The unequal distribution of the vote constituted a more acceptable and more readily approved breakwater against the masses. In the liberal democracies, it served to give a greater electoral weight to the rural areas and the small towns, which attached more importance to the established order and were easier to manipulate, while it weakened the large cities, which were more liberal and more subversive. The system had been developed in Britain with the rotten boroughs. Later, it spread to continental Europe and America in other forms. In 1940, 56 percent of the population of the United States lived in urban areas, which had only 135 of the 435 members of the House of Representatives; there was undoubtedly less inequality between 1870 and 1939, but it was, nevertheless, considerable. It existed also in the state legislatures. The federal system aggravated it in the Senate, where each state is represented by two Senators, regardless of its population; the underpopulated states, which are generally agrarian, have a considerable advantage. In Europe, the recruiting of the upper chambers is often quite the opposite of egalitarian (for example, in France); bicameralism represents a means of weakening universal suffrage.

Indirect suffrage made it possible to obtain similar results. The members of electoral colleges are usually professional politicians or notables who have some respect for the economic oligarchy and who are closer to its views than the citizenry as a whole. The fact that the members of the American Senate were designated by the state legislatures until 1913 made it less democratic and more docile. The election of the French Senate by provincial and municipal councilors leads to the same result, aggravated by the preponderance of rural electors; in this case, indirect suffrage is combined with nonegalitarian suffrage. The selection of the president of the United States by presidential electors was established for the same reason; the founding fathers did not want an election by direct suffrage, because they distrusted democracy, as did the French Constituent Assembly of 1791. To their way of thinking, the electors were meant to constitute a college of elders, above the disputes of the masses. The evolution of the political parties altered the system, so that the presidential electors voted according to their party affiliations, and the citizens chose them on the same basis.

The machinery of candidate selection made it possible to contain popular pressures in another way. In the end, it represented the most frequent and the most effective breakwater against universal suffrage. In all elections, the people chose only among the candidates previously placed on the ballot by the political organizations. It was enough for the economic oligarchy to control these to make certain that the electoral game was played exclusively by people who had its approval in varying degrees. Such, almost without exception, was the case in the liberal democracies. The structure of parties staffed by professionals, lacking any popular base, and financed almost entirely by businessmen does not allow a politician to attain an independent position. Candidates not supported by the political organizations have hardly any resources for propaganda and are almost always defeated, except in rural counties. The conflicts over the method of selection of candidates by the parties stem largely from the conflicts within the ruling oligarchy, for example, between local businessmen and national pressure groups.

However, a popular movement for the purpose of obtaining a more direct participation by the citizens in the choice of candidates appeared at the end of the nineteenth century; in Europe, there was the creation of parties for the masses, in the United States there was the establishment of primaries. The mass parties are open to all citizens. All the members take part in the nomination of candidates, either directly in general assemblies (for elections within a narrow local area) or by designating—on the basis of proportional representation—delegates who afterward sit in a party congress. The American primaries are preelections in which all citizens are invited to choose the party candidates for the final elections. In most primaries, which are called "closed," each voter indicates the party with which he is affiliated; the primary approximates the system of the mass party. But this is not a matter of a real, permanent affiliation entailing the obligation to support the organization, to pay regular dues, and so on; one simply declares that one is voting for such-and-such a party in such-and-such a primary election.

Mass parties and primaries have scarcely realized the hopes that they aroused. In the party assemblies and congresses, the members or their representatives usually designate the candidates proposed by the leadership of the party. In the Socialist and Communist parties, at least, the party oligarchies are independent of the economic oligarchy, although social democracy was quickly enough assimilated into the capitalist system. In the American primaries, the voters are also hobbled in their choices by the party committees, which are not independent of the economic oligarchy. The committees present several candidates instead of one; but they all enjoy the confidence of the organization and the oligarchy. The choice of the citizens is exercised only within this narrow framework. It is rare that independent individuals succeed in compelling recognition, even in the rare states with "open" primaries, in which the voter does not have to disclose the party whose candidates he designates and does not have to vote only for candidates from one party.

The liberal democracies have surrounded universal suffrage with sufficient safeguards to prevent it from interfering with the ruling oligarchy. Moreover, the Constitutional Convention in Philadelphia and the Constituent Assembly in Paris had misinterpreted the situation, as a result of their fear of the subversive effects of a popular vote. In actual practice, universal suffrage has proved to be an admirable instrument of social stabilization. Most people are naturally conservative—even those buried in wretched existences—because they fear that upheaval would make them still more miserable. Incessant propaganda from parties and popular organizations is required to make the workers struggle vigorously against capitalist society; for all that, the majority does not have a revolutionary attitude in the industrialized nations. Mass risings in anger that lead to overthrow of the government are rare in history. By allowing all the citizens to express themselves—or by giving them the illusion that they are expressing themselves—universal suffrage also fulfills the function of a safety valve, which makes such crises even less frequent.

In any event, the liberal democracies have protected themselves against those crises by efficacious techniques of repression. Some were born of private initiative; for example, the organization of employer-financed unions charged with breaking strikes, whose members Frenchmen call *jaunes* (literally, *yellows*, the equivalent of the British *blackleg* or the American *scab*). Some businessmen organized variants of company militias, made up of men prepared to do anything for the purpose of maintaining order and silencing agitators, who could be spotted by means of internal espionage services. These methods have been used on both sides of the Atlantic, with a greater development in the United States. In that country, the tradition of expeditious summary justice rendered by the local community outside the limits of the law—lynching—has occasionally been turned against people who obstructed the economic oligarchy, notably in the South. Some industrial corporations have not hesitated to use violence to attain their ends, for example, in the construction of railways.

This private repression is marginal in contrast to the public repression organized by political power. The old autocratic systems depended heavily on the strength of their police and their armies. Liberal democracy has not hesitated to utilize both when the dominance of the economic oligarchy appeared to be threatened. In May 1871, with appalling violence, it put down the Paris Commune, which had respected political liberalism by organizing pluralistic elections, but which threatened the capitalist system. In more recent times, other Western nations have broken strikes or demonstrations thought to be seditious. The military has rarely hesitated to take part in this fashion in the repression of popular movements. But the army personified values other than profit-seeking and the supremacy of money—honor, courage, and dedication. In Europe before 1914, the officers were often of aristocratic origin and did not care much for businessmen or capitalism; but they firmly believed that only a forceful demeanor could preserve civilization and the established order.

Another group not much inclined by tradition to support the leaders of the business world—the judiciary—became an auxiliary of the repressive system that upheld its influence. Statute and common law, in general, are firm upholders of property and the authority of employers. In some countries, a worker had to offer evidence in support of his own testimony before a court, while the employer was taken at his word. In general, the courts exacerbated instead of attenuating these prejudicial procedural provisions, thus becoming the instruments of the economic oligarchy. Many examples of such treatment can be cited, including the union members and workers' leaders imprisoned without cause, to say nothing of those intemperately condemned to death, of whom Sacco and Vanzetti in the United States are among the most famous.

The Assimilation of the Masses and Consensus

The economic oligarchy's control of the means of education and information represents a more indirect, more subtle, and more discreet method of containing the mass of the people. It has been employed on a large scale. In it, contraint and persuasion meet. The task is one of persuasion; but it is accomplished through a disguised constraint. The child is obliged to submit to the education imposed on him; the adult can only with difficulty avoid being conditioned by the press, by information in general, by the overall environment, by the morality preached by religion, and so on. In the liberal democracies, the economic oligarchy controls all of these, either directly or indirectly.

Direct control of the press was particularly strong: newspapers depended almost entirely on businessmen until the beginning of the twentieth century, when Socialist parties began to establish their own papers. In contrast, direct control of education was limited. In the United States the oligarchy subsidized the best universities, but these accounted for only a minority of the students. In Europe, it subsidized many schools, but it did so by indirect means. Through religious organizations it exercised influence on private education, and through its control of the local representatives and the state it influenced the public schools. Even the lay schools in the French Third Republic inculcated respect for property and the authority of the businessman. But the most effective means of assimilating the people used by the business community before World War II was the support of the church. The subsidies given to the religious organizations played only a minor role in this alliance between Christianity and capitalism. It was based upon more fundamental and broader interests, and it held true for both Catholicism and Protestantism, even though each reacted differently to the expansion of liberal ideology. Religion and the economic oligarchy joined forces against socialism.

In general, religions are against revolutionary movements. Preaching that what matters is the life to come, religion tends to withdraw from earthly existence and to urge resignation. More important, Catholicism and Protestantism were to be reunited in the defense of private property, free enterprise, and the authority of employers, all of which they regarded as being matters of natural law—in other words, matters in conformance with the order of Providence.

Both branches of Christianity went much further in their support of capitalism. They were embarrassed by the latent contradiction between their basic principles of unselfishness, indifference to worldly possession, charity, and brotherhood and the fundamental rules of the liberal economic system—merciless competition, self-centered profit-seeking, the rule of money—in spite of the partial reconciliation arrived at by some Protestant sects. To escape this contradiction, they relegated the essential rules of their social morality to the background and thrust into the foreground another aspect of that morality: the repression of sexuality. This transposition of interdicts from the economic to the fleshly realm had begun long before. It was already in evidence during the feudal era, and from the nineteenth century on, it acquired much greater force.

The "sin of the flesh" appears three times in the Gospels: in Christ's dialogue with the woman of Samaria, in the questions put to him concerning the woman taken in adultery, and in the figure of Mary Magdalene, the prostitute. Each time the lesson is one of compassion and understanding. The tone and the substance are completely different from those dealing with the rich, for whom "it is more difficult to enter into the Kingdom of Heaven than for a camel to pass through the eye of a needle"; or with the need to renounce worldly possessions to gain eternal life, the glorification of poverty, and the fundamental principles of altruism: "Love one another . . . Thou shalt love thy neighbor as thyself." The Gospels never neglected purity of morals and freedom from desire. But they clearly subordinated these to charity—that is, to the love of one's neighbor.

To support capitalism—in other words, a social system based on the selfishness of personal profit—Christianity of the nineteenth century reversed the priorities: it gave prime importance to virginity in girls, to continence in boys, to fidelity in spouses; less emphasis was placed on brotherhood and charity. The anathema against sex replaced the anathema against money. Extramarital relations became a thousand times more serious than exploitation of one's fellow man, employee, or customer. At the beginning of the Middle Ages, Christianity had tried to make a stand against the excesses of feudalism. It did not make the same stand against the excesses of capitalism at the beginning of the industrial era. On the contrary, it contributed to thoses excesses, with the exception of a few groups of Social Christians, who were a very small minority.

The control of the means of education and information by the economic oligarchy as well as the support given to it by the church played an important role in the development of a consensus in its favor. But this was secondary to the role played by liberal ideology itself. By linking, even in terms of the vocabulary used, individual and political liberties with the economic freedoms associated with capitalism, liberal ideology produced a formidable rationalization of capitalism and of the role played by businessmen in the society. In the United States, the linkage of political ideology and capitalism was not contested, and the system of liberal values legitimated the domination of the oligarchy. Elections, representative assemblies, judicial guarantees, freedom of expression—the basic elements of political pluralism—could not be separated from free enterprise, the search for profit, the private ownership of the means of production, and respect for businessmen. They were two sides of the same coin.

The situation was different in Europe, where the economic aspect and the political aspect of liberalism aroused different reactions in different groups. The universal character of the political principles of the Western system attracted most citizens, but not the conservative aristocrats, who remained wedded to the past. Compared with the preexisting institutions based on heredity and privilege, governmental absolutism, lack of freedom, and inequality, liberal institutions represented immense progress, even for the mass of the people. Even if they gave the people more power in theory than in practice, parliaments, elections, and civil liberties appeared preferable to a system which ignored them. It was difficult for the leaders of the revolutionary Socialist parties, advocates of the dictatorship of the proletariat, to convince the people of the contrary.

But the economic system—capitalism—did not receive the same acceptance in Europe that it did in the United States. The power of the businessman was never considered to be as legitimate as that of the elected representatives. The conservative aristocrats, who generally rejected the political aspect of liberalism, did favor capitalism, because it was an efficient means of exploiting the land. But the Socialist workers rejected capitalism; and the later development of socialism made the masses conscious of the material exploitation that they were suffering, and this recognition led them to reject the economic aspect of liberalism.

But even those who reject the linking of capitalism and political liberties are forced to accept the first as the price for the second while waiting for full democracy to develop. Marxist theory encouraged this attitude by regarding bourgeois liberalism as a necessary precursor of socialism. In addition, the material successes of capitalism between 1870 and 1914 weakened the hostility of those who were opposed to either the economic or the political aspect of liberalism. The workers found that even while the entrepreneurs profited they themselves gained better working conditions, and thus, with few exceptions, they favored the continuation of the liberal system. As capitalism enriched the conservative aristocrats, their opposition to political liberalism lessened, became more and more theoretical, less and less actual. Thus, in the end, the powers of the oligarchy were violently and radically disputed by only a few. In the end, although the European acceptance of liberalism did not approach a consensus of the American type, adherence to liberalism was widespread in Europe.

Chapter Six

The Crisis of Liberal Democracy (1918-1939)

In 1918, liberal democracy seemed stronger than ever. The victory over the Central Powers was its triumph. The chief victors were also the leading practitioners of the Western system, the first to adopt it after they had invented it: Great Britain, the United States, France. The rulers in business suits in Paris, London, and Washington had conquered the rulers in uniform in Berlin and Vienna. Parliamentary institutions took over new territories. They were embraced by the Weimar Republic and the new nations of Central Europe. They were even transplanted onto the international scene through the League of Nations.

But reality did not match these appearances. War itself contravenes the principles of democracy. Military victory depends on force of arms, not on free discussion and electoral choice; it is imposed on the vanquished as autocratic governments are imposed on peoples. To triumph, the liberal nations had had to anesthetize their institutions. Parliaments had barely any part in decisions; civilian officials were in practice dominated by the military. At every level of society, violence had supplanted persuasion, discipline had thrust aside debate, nationalist passion had overwhelmed the critical spirit. It would take a long time for these habits to die.

The new democracies turned out to be very frail. In Central Europe, liberal institutions were grafted onto quasi-feudal societies. Subjected to the domination of great landowners, hemmed in by backward, conservative clergies, illiterate, and devoid of political consciousness, the masses of the people could hardly affect decisions or freely choose their representatives. De facto dictatorships were very soon established everywhere except Czechoslovakia, where industrial Bohemia, with its liberal traditions, preserved an island of democracy, an outpost of the Western system, which otherwise had fallen back on its pre-1914 positions.

Even if circumstances had been more favorable, the socioeconomic structures would undoubtedly have brought about this retreat. In any case, the ambience was not propitious to liberal democracy between the two world wars. The obstacles to reconstruction in the 1920s and then the frightful depression of the 1930s battered it hard. Fear of Soviet communism drove the ruling classes to authoritarian solutions. This pressure was reinforced by the weaknesses of the parliaments. Liberalism—economic and political—seemed to have been left behind by events. The new generation was rejecting it. On the eve of the Second World War, the Western system seemed very weak and severely threatened.

Crisis in Society

Two successive crises arose in the West between 1918 and 1939, the first in the 1920s, the second in the 1930s. They were quite different. The postwar crisis was complex and multiform. It progressed unevenly in different countries, assuming individual forms in each. It was a mixture of the economic, the social, the political, the ideological, and the psychological in proportions that shifted with time and place. It affected Europe predominantly. The United States, on the other hand, was enjoying a major expansion after a period of recession. The depression that erupted in 1929 had a more clearly defined shape. Here, the basic part was played by the economy, although the consequences made themselves felt in every sphere. The impetus came from the United States, where the depression was the worst. Step by step, it spread to the rest of the world. Some students regarded it as one of the cyclical crises described by economists; but it exceeded all its predecessors in its extent and its intensity.

We will deal here not with these two crises themselves but only with their effects on the Western system. In this connection, there are two essential elements, around which the rest can be assembled. On the one hand, capitalism seemed to have been cast adrift. The growth, the energy, the efficiency that it had evidenced between 1870 and 1914, in spite of periodic recessions, gave way to impotence, to rigidity, to paralysis. Thus, the economic foundation of liberal democracy was weakened and menaced. The political base was also affected. The 1917 revolution and the accession of communism in the Soviet Union revived

92

the fear of "Reds," which gained new vigor. Class conflict intensified abruptly, and consensus flagged.

Convulsions of Capitalism

The first disruption of capitalism was the war, which gave it a violent impetus in certain areas. Wartime capitalism demonstrated its faculty for adaptation and its vigor, even though its expansion was brought about by state controls rather than by competition and demand. The need for weapons, which was paramount and imperative, produced a considerable measure of growth in certain kinds of enterprises. Large investments were made quickly, and huge profits were gathered subsequently, thus making further investments possible. In spite of all the damage done by the war, the capacity for production was much greater than before the war.

The destruction was great, though very unevenly distributed. France was the hardest hit, suffering at the same time a vast loss of life and tremendous property losses. Germany, too, suffered a high death toll, but virtually no destruction of property. Great Britain, too, was spared in this respect, and her manpower toll was also lower. The United States was untouched by property damage, and its human casualties were relatively minor. The neutral nations (the Netherlands, Sweden, Switzerland) were untouched. It must be remembered that it was the young, who were thrown into the front lines, who suffered the worst; 20 percent of the men between twenty and forty years of age in France and Germany were killed or seriously wounded, a toll that cut deeply into the working population. Similarly, European machinery had lost much of its productivity, as a result of obsolescence and the inability to replace worn-out machinery during the war years.

The war had upset the balance of power in the West. By destroying one another, the nations of the Old World had brought on its decline and thrust the United States into a leading position. Before 1914, America was Europe's debtor; in 1918, Europe owed the United States four billion dollars for enormous purchases of munitions and equipment. The United States had expanded and modernized its industrial arsenal to meet these demands, and it had taken over the foreign customers and the commercial networks that the Europeans had abandoned to concentrate their efforts on the war. Nonetheless, the United

States suffered a severe slump in 1920-21, though this was caused primarily by its trade policy.

The halt in arms orders could have been counterbalanced by the growth of civilian demand. Europe's needs were infinite in this area, for purposes of reconstruction and to satisfy the consumer needs of people chafing to enjoy life after five years of privation and sacrifice. But the American government cut off the credits that it had granted to the Old World for war purposes. At first, the Europeans continued to buy; but this led to such a weakening in their currency values that they had to stop. This in turn led to a slump in the sales of American goods, which brought on a drop in prices and increases in unsold inventories, bankruptcies (a hundred thousand in 1921), and unemployment (amounting to five million persons in the same year).

By the end of 1921, the recession had begun to ease, and the American economy embarked on a phase of growth and prosperity based essentially on the expansion of domestic demand. The United States withdrew into itself and embraced isolationism. Following Henry Ford's example, industry adopted a policy of high wages, creating purchasing power that assured product consumption. Real wages of factory and white-collar workers rose on the average by a third between 1921 and 1929. At the same time, installment buying mounted. The United States began to be a "consumer society": automobiles, telephones, radios were common in the majority of homes, and advertising became the mentor of economic policy.

The postwar depression was longer and sharper in Europe, which did not recover until about 1925 and was left enfeebled. Britain devalued her currency, thus injuring her exports and her production. The collapse of the mark in 1923 had shaken German society to its roots; industrial expansion was very impressive, but it was founded on short-term foreign credits, the cessation of which could lead to disaster. Unemployment and farm problems were major concerns on both sides of the Atlantic. From 1921 to 1929, Britain consistently had an absolute minimum of one million unemployed. The percentage in Germany hovered near 15; even in 1929, a year of high prosperity, it was still 13.6. The unemployment figure in the United States, during this period, averaged two million; at no time was it less than one and a half million.

Though the United States suffered less than Europe from unemployment, its agricultural problems were greater. Western farmers in general had difficulty in selling their products, and their scale of living was dropping. The situation in the United States was serious; prices of wheat fell by 50 percent between 1919 and 1928, of corn by 80 percent, of cotton by 40 percent, of rice by 37 percent. Farmers represented a quarter of the population, but, in 1927, they received only 8.8 percent of the national income, in contrast to 16 percent in 1919. Capitalism's inability to organize the production and distribution of farm products and to guarantee full employment made a dramatic impression on the popular mind. The prosperity that preceded the great depression hid the permanence of the crisis in many areas.

Nevertheless, the famous "Black Thursday"—October 24, 1929—when stock-market prices disintegrated in New York, was a decisive turning point in the postwar period. The liberal economic system was thrown into an unprecedented chaos. Industrial output fell off sharply. Unemployment rose to unheard-of figures: in the United States, in 1932, it ranged from 11.4 to 14.7 million, and it never fell below 7 million until the Second World War. Germany had 3.8 million unemployed in December 1930, and more than 5 million in 1931-32. Great Britain had 2.6 million in 1931. Business failures were numerous, and small firms were swallowed up by big companies and financial corporations. Thousands of farm properties in the United States fell into the hands of the banks and lending companies that held the mortgages on them. One company alone foreclosed on more than seven thousand farms in Montana, and 15.6 percent of the farmers in Oklahoma and 11.9 percent of those in Iowa were evicted. The banks merged the properties, and the former owners were driven out. This is the tragedy that John Steinbeck depicted in *The Grapes of Wrath*.

Liberal economists viewed this cataclysm as one of those cyclical crises about which they had long been elaborating theories—theories, however, that were contradictory. In fact, it was a structural crisis brought on by the transition from classic capitalism to contemporary neoclassic capitalism. Productive capacity was reaching the level of the latter in the most developed countries (the United States and Germany), where the size of firms, the potential of their machinery, and the evolution of credit were close to today's levels. But the overall organization of production did not yet exist; the consolidation and reorganization of producing companies by holding corporations was still limited, the management of the economy through government action was unknown, the control of consumption through advertising and the mass media was still unborn.

Given the dimensions of the crisis, state intervention was demonstrably necessary. The strongest champions of free enterprise were clamoring for it. In October 1931, the Chamber of Commerce of the United States called for the adoption of "a national program of production and distribution" (the Harriman Committee). Action by public authorities varied considerably from country to country; but everywhere they intervened to restrict competition, regulate prices and wages, organize production, embark on major public works, develop public sectors in the economy—all of which were completely contrary to capitalism. In the United States, the New Deal was the first coordinated experiment in planned economy, based on renewal of the pace of production by injecting purchasing power (wage increases, subsidies to farmers, high pensions for veterans, and so on) and on systems of restricting competition (industrial agreements, including interoccupational accords, regulation of banking and securities exchanges, planned and reduced farm production, and so on). France under the Popular Front developed a program of the same kind.

Officially, the Western nations regarded these steps as being consistent with capitalism; they contended that such measures tended to restore the normal working of competition and market mechanisms. But the fact that this normal competition and these market mechanisms could not recover by themselves was a direct contradiction of the basic principle of economic liberalism. The theory of the automatic regulation of production and consumption, the keystone of the Western system, could not withstand the great depression. Even when its material effects had vanished and an economic recovery had begun, the psychological effect remained. Capitalism was laid open to challenge by the depression of the 1930s. Many of its followers lost their faith and went in search of a "third way" between it and the socialism that they continued to loathe. This search was the source of theories of corporatism, planned or directed economy, and so forth. They were the instruments of vigorous challenge to one of the fundamental premises of liberal ideology.

The Panic of the Respectable

The Russian Revolution of 1917 strewed panic through the economic oligarchy and the middle classes—the fear of bolshevism. Socialism had aroused a similar fright in the beginning. In 1848, Tocqueville compared the dread of socialism with the terror that gripped the residents of the Gallic-Roman towns, who trembled before the advance of the barbarians. The fear of socialism had gradually diminished in spite of the growth of Socialist parties or, perhaps, even because of it. The British Labourites and the German and Scandinavian Social Democrats established powerful organizations. They announced their desire to erect a new society. But they moved within the framework of the established order, taking legal rather than revolutionary paths. They had recognition, they were serious, society had become accustomed to them. They seemed to have been incorporated into liberal democracy, and so, indeed, they were, more or less, in spite of their ideology and their rhetoric.

Everything changed after 1917. Now socialism seemed possible, because it had been initiated. Now there was a Socialist country, a Socialist model; proof existed that a society could live without capitalism. This revived hope among the proletarians of many countries; but it also aroused fear among managing directors, owners of the means of production, the middle classes. This fear was all the stronger because initially the Soviet Revolution seemed infectious. The *cordon sanitaire* that was erected around the Soviet Union did not prevent the organized spread of communism through the Third International established by the Russians in 1919 and ruled by them with an iron hand. The Moscow experiment fascinated even those whom it frightened.

The panic of the respectable was the sharper because bolshevism had not been kind to the former ruling classes. It had "liquidated" the capitalists, and it resumed doing so after the fleeting respite of the New Economic Policy. The bourgeoisie was far less susceptible to incorporation into the Socialist order than the aristocracy had been to assimilation into the capitalist order. Of course, the violence of the Russian Revolution has been exaggerated; a good proportion of the middle-level personnel of the old order finally succeeded in finding a place in the new one. But these men's situation was much more difficult than it had been. Above all, very little was known of their restoration in the Western nations, which concentrated their attention on the swarm of emigrants fleeing the revolution. The European and American middle classes trembled at the notion that one day they, too, might thus be driven out of their homelands.

The first years after the 1918 armistice seemed to justify these fears. A "Red" republic was set up in Bavaria, and all Germany seemed to be about to swing over in the direction of Moscow. In the other Western countries, there was a mounting wave of workers' demands in 1919 and 1920. Trade-union membership increased, eight million in the United Kingdom, two million in the Confédération générale de travail in France, four million in the American Federation of Labor (AFL). Numerous social conflicts broke out, particularly in the form of major strikes in mines and textile factories in Britain, in coal mines and steel mills in the United States, and so on. Governments were frequently compelled to give in; the eight-hour day was established in France, and Britain adopted unemployment insurance.

The reaction was swift. The Communist republic in Budapest was overthrown with the help of the Romanian and Czechoslovak armies, and it was replaced with a reactionary government that instituted a fearsome repression. The capitalist system was restored throughout Germany, thanks to the support of the army. Resistance to strikes was organized. In March 1920, the French government refused to negotiate and crushed popular demonstrations. The British mine strike of April-June 1921 ended in failure. As early as the end of 1919, the American coal and steel strikes had been broken. Worker agitation in the United States was resumed in the 1920-21 depression; but it was put down with great harshness. Large companies instituted company unions, which they controlled; they recruited private police forces and strikebreakers. In a few years, the AFL lost half its members. The European unions, too, were losing momentum.

Repression was made easier by the accession of communism in Russia, which had weakened the labor movement rather than strengthened it. Socialist parties and unions divided over the question of the Third International. Sometimes the split would take place within an existing organization, which remained ostensibly united, though it was torn by factional battles. More often, conflict led to schism, a Communist party or union being established in competition with a Social Democratic group. Relations between these groups became increasingly strained. The Communists looked on the Socialists as tools of the bourgeoisie, "social traitors." They in turn regarded the Communists as dangerous agitators. This split in the labor movement made its operations less effective. From 1921 to roughly 1939, liberal democracy was not really threatened in the West; there was neither a time nor a country in which the accession of socialism was a possibility.

But the rich and the middle classes thought that liberal democracy was in danger. To them, the return of social peace seemed a mere temporary lull. The great fear of "Reds" was still latent; it was always enough to drive to the right those moderate voters who determine the victory of one side or the other. Thus, while dissidence was weakening the labor movement, the dread of an imaginary socialism was gaining strength and fostering the defense of the established order. Throughout the West conservative governments were to hold power almost constantly throughout the 1920s and to use it in a rigorous fashion, opposing reforms and resorting to repression.

The Republicans returned to power in the United States in 1921 (through the election of November 1920) and were not unseated until 1933. While economic development was modernizing the country, a profound psychological and economic reaction was evolving. The nation turned inward on itself, following President Harding's 1920 slogan: "Defend America first, think of America first, love America first." To keep out political agitators and persons of Latin or Oriental origin, legislation enacted in 1921 and 1924 cut down immigration to a great degree (700,000 immigrants in 1919, 150,000 in 1925, 200,000 Italian immigrants a year between 1900 and 1910, 5,000 after 1924). To preserve the purity of the white race, the Ku Klux Klan was revived. To preserve public morals, a 1919 law prohibited the use of alcoholic beverages throughout the country, leading to vast corruption and crime. To preserve civic virtue and fight communism, the American Legion, a veterans' organization, launched a crusade. The contrast between the modernity of the economy and the archaism of politics reached its apogee in the laws by which some states prohibited the teaching of Darwin's theories on the evolution of the species on the ground that they ran counter to the Bible. The mentality that led to Galileo's condemnation by the church came back to life in the era and the country in which science was forging ahead.

The conservatives' tenure in Europe was less firm. For a time, the left held power in Britain and France after the 1924 elections; in both cases, it was paralyzed by its allies from the center (the Liberals in Britain, the Radicals in France), who tended to side with the conservatives rather than with the "Reds." In Germany, the coalition Weimar governments (Socialists, Catholic Centrists, and Liberals) slid progressively rightward; the Socialists had to yield control of the cabinet and the major ministries to the Catholics (1920) and then to the Liberals (1922). The election of Marshal von Hindenburg to the presidency in 1925 emphasized the return to traditional conservatism. Everywhere the dominance of the right was accompanied by a policy of resistance to workers' organizations (limitation on the right to strike in Britain in 1926, the law curbing the privileges of trade unions, the refusal to carry out land reform in Germany in 1919, the weakness of the factory councils set up in 1920, the repression of trade-union activity in France).

In the decade before the great depression, the class struggle seemed less acute than it had been just after the war. Was it really diminishing, or was it assuming less obvious forms? The question is not easily answered. The conservative, repressive policy of the governments in power probably incited resentments that grew in depth. The river flowed below ground and was swollen by new tributaries as it bided its time until it could come to the surface again. The crisis of the 1930s forced it to break through into the open.

The depression afforded a measurable momentum to the class struggle, a momentum much greater than that which followed in the wake of the war. This time, capitalism was not menaced from without by the emergence of a Socialist state. It was being eroded from within by its own incapacity to function. Liberal economics had lost its basic justification. For almost a century, it had experienced a virtually continuous expansion, in spite of some periodic recessions. It had increased the material goods available to mankind. Undoubtedly, their distribution was still inequitable. But the cake was now bigger and each could have a little larger slice.

Capitalism was paralyzed in the 1930s. Production dropped. Inventories piled up, because there were no buyers; yet millions of people who needed goods lacked the means to buy them. The tremendous rise in unemployment attested to the absurdity of the system, as did the coffee that was burned as fuel for locomotives, the wheat that was put to nonfood uses, the crops that could no longer be planted, while men were without food. How could the workers, thus directly affected, retain any faith in the liberal economy? Socialism's attraction for them was the greater on this very score, in spite of the faults of Stalinism, which at the time—since they were farther away and better concealed— were less well known than those of capitalism. It was only the lack of jobs that kept down workers' demands, for the employed were afraid that they would be dismissed if they struck and that the unemployed would get their jobs.

The impotence of the liberal economy repelled the workers, who had begun to be assimilated by it before 1914. It thrust the rich and the middle classes into a situation that, in certain respects, was worse. Psychologically, they were trapped in a dead end. They were afraid that capitalism could no longer function, and it was essential to their existence; the accession of socialism would reduce them to the level of wage-earners, which they thoroughly loathed. Moreover the economic impotence of plutodemocracy was made worse for them by its political impotence; in the face of the danger into which liberal society was plunged in the 1930s, its fragile parliamentary institutions seemed hardly capable of preserving the established order.

Crisis in Political Institutions

Liberal political institutions have never worked very well. Anatole France said of democracy: "I forgive it for governing badly because it governs so little." The mediocrity of American politicians, with very few exceptions, was in dramatic contrast to the capacities of American businessmen. In Europe, the traditions of the aristocracy and the sense of the state generally gave the ruling classes a more impressive veneer, but what lay beneath was not much different. There is no evidence, however, that earlier systems worked any better. The perspective of history blurs the grays and preserves only the bright colors; many of the "great men" of the past seem great to us only because we barely know them. Count Oxenstiern, the eighteenth-century chancellor of Sweden, said to his son: "If only you knew by what stupid people the world is governed." In 1920, the historian, Jacques Bainville, told a pretty woman who was trying to persuade him that the old monarchy had governed better than the Third Republic: "Madame, things have always gone very badly."

Between 1870 and 1914, liberal democracy had, on the whole, worked much better than all of the systems that preceded it. To prove the point, French republicans, after the war, had devised the ingenious commentaries of Louis XIX. If this (mythical) descendant of the Bourbons had ascended the throne of his fathers at an early age, on September 2, 1870, and remained on it until 1919, performing exactly the same work as the Third Republic and within the same period, it would have been he and not Louis XIV whom historians would call "the Great." Taking a conquered country from which Alsace and Lorraine had been severed, which had been torn apart by the dreadful revolution of the Paris Commune, which was weakened and humiliated, he would have restored harmony among its citizens, rehabilitated its finances, developed its economy, won the second greatest colonial empire in the world, recovered the lost provinces, and led a coalition of free peoples to victory in the greatest war in history. One can envisage a similar glory for a monarch enthroned in Washington from 1865 to 1919. Did not Victoria's reign in Britain afford her contemporaries the same impression of greatness?

Between 1919 and 1939, in contrast, liberal democracy functioned much worse than the average of all political systems. The crisis of its institutions, like that of society, went through two paroxysms, one immediately after the war, the other after 1929. There was no reason for surprise, since the second derived in part from the first. The lull between them was not universal. The German currency catastrophe of 1923 thoroughly rocked the country and the system. The less serious French monetary crisis of 1926 brought executive law-making into the nation's life, thus profoundly altering the constitution. The British elections of 1923 and 1924 changed the party system, the foundations of British parliamentarianism. Except in the United States, where the years between 1921 and 1929 seemed a return to a prewar golden age, the institutional crisis was more protracted than the social one.

The Forms the Crisis Took

The instability of governments and parliaments was the spectacular aspect of the crisis in Western institutions, the form that made the most vivid impression on popular thinking. Obviously it was true only of Europe, since the American presidential system allows for neither the fall of a cabinet nor the dissolution of a parliament. Before the war, France had been almost the only Western nation that experienced frequent cabinet crises: the average life of a French government between 1870 and 1914 was nine months. After the war, the mortality rose: between 1918 and 1939 the average cabinet lasted only six months. This instability spread to other countries of western Europe. German governments between 1919 and 1933 lasted eight months, on an average. While Belgian governments averaged eighteen months between the two world wars, this was less than half the pre-1914 average of three years and nine months.

Even Britain experienced governmental instability between 1922 and 1924 and again between 1929 and 1931. Because of the workings of dissolution, this led to parliamentary instability. The legislature elected in 1922 lasted a year, its successor less than eleven months. The legislature elected in 1929 survived less than two and a half years. In Weimar Germany, the instability of the Reichstag became chronic after 1928. The legislatures chosen in 1928 and 1930 lasted two years each; those elected in July and November of 1932 lasted five months each. In the two years before Adolf Hitler's accession to power, the parliamentary engine was totally seized, and power was held by cabinets that had no majorities in the Reichstag.

The impotence of governments and parliaments, however, was more serious than their instability, which at times was more apparent than real. France under the Third Republic was the perfect proof of the accuracy of the maxim that "ministries pass but the ministers remain." The same men appeared in cabinet after cabinet after cabinet, whether in the same or in different posts; this persistence of ministers was in inverse proportion to the longevity of the ministries.[1] Even when individuals were replaced by others, the new men most often resembled the old; they came from the same parties or represented the same policies. It was not difficult to understand the witticism that ran through Paris with every change of cabinet: "Plus ca change, plus c'est la même chose"—"The more it changes, the more it's the same."

---

1. Cf. J. Ollé-Laprune, *La stabilité des ministres sous la illieme République (1879-1940) (Ministerial Stability in the Third Republic [1879-1940])* (Paris, 1962).

What difference did it make whether the changes were real or apparent, if every government evidenced the same inability to govern? Immediately after the war, and particularly during the Great Depression, all governments made more or less this same impression in the West. Sometimes their impotence resulted from parliamentary obstructionism; they lacked majorities, and the legislators rebuffed all their initiatives. This was the case in France and in Germany in the 1930s. More often, the measures adopted did not produce the hoped-for results. Political institutions were spinning in a void; they had no foothold on reality, no impact on society. This phenomenon was general in the West in the early years of the Great Depression. It survived in the sphere of foreign policy, where the democracies' behavior in confrontation with the dictatorships was deplorable until 1939 and even until June of 1940.

Nevertheless, the system evolved self-regulatory mechanisms that curbed the instability and the impotence of political institutions. In a general way, governments tended to encroach on parliamentary prerogatives, particularly in legislating by decree. In this way, it was possible to make decisions and institute reforms without having a majority or to save a majority from having to assume direct responsibility for unpopular measures. In Germany, the executive acted through presidential decrees by virtue of Article 48 of the Weimar Constitution, which dealt with states of emergency. In the United States, President Roosevelt increased his interventions in the economy within the framework of his normal powers, which occasionally, in the opinion of the Supreme Court, he exceeded.

The most original reform, which was also the most thoroughgoing, was undertaken in France in the form of decree-laws. Used during the war alongside legal methods, the procedure had been introduced into certain European constitutions after 1918. The French parliament first resorted to it in 1924, by delegating its own legislative power to the government for a limited time and in a limited domain. Within these limits, the executive could issue decrees having the force of law—in other words, it could act in legislative matters and, possibly, amend existing legislation. Some legal authorities questioned whether a parliament may thus delegate its power to legislate, which is not a right at its disposal but a duty that it is obligated to perform. These objections were pushed aside and the procedure became a matter of custom. Parliament, however, reserved to itself the right to ratify the decree-laws issued by the government. In actuality, the fact that parliament did not abrogate them was sufficient to keep them in force under the principle that silence is tantamount to consent. Decree-laws were used in 1926, 1934, 1935, 1937, 1938, and 1939. In the twenty-six months immediately preceding the war, they were used during thirteen months, or exactly half the period. Most of the important measures adopted in France in the 1930s took the form of decree-laws.

The personalization of power was another form of self-regulation in the system. It already existed in some liberal nations, notably in the United States, by way of the presidential system, and in Great Britain, through the authority of the leader of the majority party. Gladstone and Disraeli had been the personifications of nineteenth-century British liberalism and conservatism. Lincoln and Theodore Roosevelt had enjoyed great prestige and authority. Personalization increased between 1914 and 1933. French parliamentarianism resorted to the appeal to a savior in 1926 (Poincaré) and 1934 (Doumergue). A legislative reform invested the prime minister with more powers. The Franklin D. Roosevelt epoch was based essentially on the authority and the personal charm of the man; he was a great contrast to the pallid presidents of the years between 1920 and 1932—Harding and Coolidge and Hoover. In Belgium, van Zeeland incarnated the battle against Léon Degrelle's fascism. In the last years of the Weimar Republic, there was an evolution in the direction of presidentialism—that is, gerater power for Field Marshall von Hindenburg. Politically incapable and intellectually failing, he was only a symbol behind which the people around him functioned; but personal power naturally is conducive to palace intrigues.

The liberal democracies have sometimes been criticized for taking over the methods of dictatorships but there is a tremendous difference between the *Führerprinzip*—the leadership principle as exemplified in Germany and enunciated by Hitler—and the authority of the liberal governors. The latter was always restricted; it was accompanied by no cult of personality; it ruled out blind, passive obedience; it could be terminated by a vote of parliament or people; it was of short duration (except in Roosevelt's case). At the same time, both fulfilled the common need to turn to the father, the savior, the exceptional man in time of trouble. This evidenced a regression toward some irrational, charismatic power fundamentally opposed to the liberal concept of an empiric, rational power.

Another self-regulatory mechanism that the Western democracies evolved between 1919 and 1934 was to be found also in the dictatorships, representation for special interests and professional organizations. It first appeared in Weimar Germany and in some of the new Central European constitutions as a means of giving the trade unions a place in the state and fostering collaboration between management and labor. The National Economic Council established in France in 1929 and elaborated in 1936 had the same objectives; furthermore, it derived its inspiration from the German Economic Council. Roosevelt's codes[2] tended rather toward organizing the various occupations to regiment production. No effort of such scope was to be found in Europe, but many nations followed similar procedures for specific economic activities. This was an approach to the corporatism so fashionable in the 1930s.

Some observers regarded this corporatism as a third road between capitalism and socialism. In actuality, it corresponded to the structure of production, in which, little by little, the large firms were dominating the market; thus, they tended to match their economic power with political power. The Fascist governments, for their part, employed corporatism to break the labor unions, which were dominated by management within the "corporations," and the parties, which were ousted from assemblies that now were founded on occupational rather than political representation. The liberal democracies exploited occupational organizations for very different ends.

The extent of the crisis in political institutions varied considerably from country to country. In this respect, three groups may be identified, though classification cannot be inflexible. Some Western nations were very seriously affected, to such a degree that democratic government foundered and gave way to dictatorship. This was the case in Central Europe—except Czechoslovakia—Italy, and Germany. These were countries in which the liberal system had been inaugurated only recently, and its roots were not adequate to stand against the gale. In Poland, Romania, Hungary, Bulgaria, and Yugoslavia, the system had never really functioned, and the fine democratic constitutions adopted

2. These codes were created under the National Industrial Recovery Act and Administration of 1933, and were invalidated by the Supreme Court in 1935.—Translator.

after the war were sheer formalities. Suffrage in Italy was very limited before 1914, and the majority of the populations took no part in politics or elections. Germany, on the other hand, had had universal male suffrage since 1871, but it operated there in a system in which the authority of the throne was still very strong; the Western system was not instituted until 1919.

A second group of nations suffered a serious crisis that rocked but did not tumble liberal institutions; France and Belgium were examples. There democracy was severely damaged materially and even more severely psychologically; parliament suffered a loss of prestige and legitimacy. Fascist parties strove for the establishment of dictatorships on the Italian or German models. In the Belgian elections of 1936, the Rexists won 12 percent of the votes cast. In Paris, the agitation by the various "leagues" culminated in the riots of February 6, 1934 (in which nineteen persons were killed and hundreds were wounded), directed against the Chamber of Deputies. Jacques Doriot's French Popular party, which at first was national and Socialist, soon drifted into national socialism, German style. Colonel de la Rocque's French Social party, though less fascistic, was hardly less antiparliamentarian.

In the other Western countries, the crisis in political institutions was more limited. In spite of economic problems, unemployment, and the paralysis of capitalism, at no time were elections or parliaments or the functions of political parties seriously challenged in these countries. An outstanding instance was the United States, where the Constitution of 1787 was still sacrosanct. There was virtually no thought of altering it, whereas the theme of state reform was widely discussed in France and Belgium. British institutions seemed as solid as the American ones. The modification of the two-party system because of the growth of the Labour party between 1930 and 1935 weakened the traditional stability of cabinets and parliaments. But this instability was limited to brief phases; at all other times, there were solid majorities.

In the small countries of northern Europe, the crisis in political institutions was hardly more serious than in Britain or the United States. The average life of a government in the Netherlands dropped from four to two years after 1918; but this term was still sufficient not to create an impression of instability. In Scandinavia, the situation was slightly less healthy; the average life of a cabinet fell to eighteen months in Sweden, to a year in Norway and Denmark. The Socialist parties in particular benefitted from the difficulties, beginning their rise to the dominant position that they hold today. Their reformist character and their devotion to democracy offered no threat to parliamentary institutions; but their growth foreshadowed changes and the advent of a new type of Western system.

The Significance of the Crisis

The crisis in institutions was obviously brought on by the crisis in society. Parliaments and elections and political parties are not ineffective by nature, as some people thought in the 1930s, since they had been effective in the half century before 1914. They became ineffective in the interval between the wars because they were no longer suited to a fundamentally altered society. The violence of the economic and social crisis, on the one hand, and the inadequate entrenchment of political liberalism, on the other, were the two basic factors, the combination of which explained the depth and the gravity of the crisis in institutions. It reached its maximum in those countries in which the depression was the worst and liberal institutions were the most fragile. The example of Germany is characteristic. That of Italy is less probative (democracy had put down feeble roots there, but Italy's social and economic crisis was not particularly acute.) In contrast, Britain is illustrative of the case of a nation where democracy was very firmly rooted and the economic crisis was less sharp.

Apart from this, the relationship between the crisis in society and the crisis in institutions was complex. Lack of confidence in parliaments and parties was seldom the consequence of lack of trust in capitalism arising out of the hardships of the postwar period and the Great Depression of the 1930s. At that time, the bonds between the liberal economy and the democratic system were not clear. The idea that the political crisis derived from the economic crisis was even less widely held, except among Marxists. The rich and the middle classes, for whom capitalism was more important than liberal institutions, tended, on the other hand, to reverse the relation and to hold parliaments responsible for the problems of industries. On both sides of the Atlantic, blame was hurled at the wastefulness of government, the demagogic appropriations of elected representatives, the burden of government payrolls on the economy. When the depression grew worse and the necessity for state intervention was imperative, the denunciations were directed against the weakness of legislatures, their fickleness, their inability to make decisions.

In various ways, democracy was made the scapegoat for the faults of a capitalism that had to be exonerated at all costs. This phenomenon of psychosocial displacement enhanced the effects of the economic crisis in the political sphere. Capitalism had been proved far more ineffectual technically than democracy, but public opinion believed the contrary. Parliaments managed to arrive at decisions, whether directly or through decree-laws. Governments were not really prevented from acting; even the most unstable, such as those of France and Weimar Germany, were endowed, on the contrary, with an accumulation of powers, and they used them. But they used them badly, just as the parliaments legislated badly—not because the political structures were defective, but because the ministers and the legislators, like the majority of the population, could not manage to extricate themselves from the orthodoxy of economic liberalism. This was something that the rich and the middle classes did not wish to recognize, because then their own existence would be jeopardized. They ascribed to political institutions the responsibility for a disaster that, in fact, was the fault of capitalism.

Elections, parliaments, and parties, then, were under attack by those who had established them in the previous century. Consensus with respect to them weakened, and so, consequently, did the legitimacy of the political system. This decline was all the greater because democratic institutions seemed too frail to sustain the established capitalist order. When that order functioned efficiently, it had no need of protection by the political system. When capitalism faltered, when its ability to produce became liable to challenge and was challenged, when confidence in it fell off, when socialism increased its pressure, a strong political system seemed required for the protection of the economic system.

As early as the 1920s, the panic that invaded the "well-to-do" after the Soviet Revolution led them to employ repression. But at that time, they had sufficient means within the framework of liberal institutions. Elections placed conservative governments in power, and they used the police and legislation against labor organizations. Only in Italy did the economic oligarchy feel so insecure that it went as far as fascism. After 1929, this tendency became general. The seriousness of the depression aroused fears that the democracies would swing to the left and socialism. The western bourgeoisie now found itself in the position of the

French bourgeoisie in 1848 and 1871 or of the Italian in 1923. In the same way, it favored a strong hand and turned its back on its liberal scruples.

The search for an authoritarian state that would take the place of parliamentary democracy arose not only from a need for social protection but also from the necessity of adapting economic structures to productive capacities. Fascism consisted not only of preserving established capitalism by force but also of transforming it, concentrating it, organizing it, regimenting it, directing it. On the one side, it brought to heel the unions and the leftist parties; on the other, it modernized capitalism by subjecting it to the required changes. The SS and Dr. Hjalmar Schacht, the German minister of national economy in the middle 1930s, were the two complementary faces of nazism.

Whenever democratic institutions seemed able to preserve the capitalist order, they were retained. In the end, they vanished only in the two Western countries in which they were the least firmly rooted, Italy and Germany. Fascist parties elsewhere gained only a limited following. After 1933, the Roosevelt experiment awakened hopes of a renewal and reinforcement of capitalism within a democratic framework that matched the preference of public opinion and the economic oligarchy, which did not favor a strong state. The growth of the European Socialist parties, paradoxically, tended in the same direction; it enhanced the likelihood of a neocapitalism adapted to the progress of the means of production, and it tended to the restoration of the Western system, as we shall see, after 1945.

Initially, the evolution of socialism had produced the opposite effect. The spread of parliamentary democracy in Europe between 1870 and 1914 paralleled that stage of history in which the conflict between conservatives and liberals had lessened sufficiently to enable them to coexist peacefully, and socialism was not then powerful enough to pose a serious threat to the capitalist order and parliamentary institutions. Thus, the attenuation of class conflict made it possible for the classes to confront each other under orderly procedures: elections, mass meetings, labor-management negotiations, and so forth. If, however, socialism becomes strong enough to cause the upper classes to fear that it may take power, the working of liberal institutions becomes much more difficult. A situation of this kind arose just after the First World

War, when the 1917 Russian Revolution sowed panic in the bourgeoisie. The Popular Front evoked a similar reaction in France in 1936.

On the whole, however, the spread of socialism between the wars did not cause the same difficulties. It became strong enough to win parliamentary majorities, to assume posts in governments, and even to lead them; but it was sufficiently integrated into liberal institutions to assure their continuing regular operation without, in any way, jeopardizing them. Indeed, its reformism tended to reassure them, for it very closely matched the evolution of the Western economy. Before 1939, Social Democracy was diffusing ideas close to those that Keynes was then developing and by which Roosevelt was animated in his New Deal. Social Democracy provided the liberal system with certain basic themes suited to adjusting it to the development of productive capacities. Thus, it exercised a strong influence on the shaping of contemporary neo-capitalism, far greater than that of the neoliberals.

The precursor function performed by the Socialist parties in the 1930s led occasionally to transitory difficulties, brief aggravations of the crisis in institutions that, in the long term, it helped resolve. In the France of 1932-1936, the coalition of the leftist parties was virtually paralyzed by the deepening of the differences between the Socialists and the Radicals. The Socialists were no longer willing to accept the Radicals' economic and financial policies, as they had done in the past. The depression led them to reject the orthodoxy that they had supported in the framework of an expanding capitalism. Their proposals were closer than those of their allies to the theories that were to become classic after 1945. The internal conflict of the leftist coalition attested not so much to a capitalism-socialism schism, though it was so conceived of at the time, as to a struggle between classic and modern capitalism.

It must be borne in mind, finally, that in certain countries the crisis in institutions assumed individual forms that derived from technical procedures. In Britain, for instance, the difficulties that afflicted the political system did not stem from the climaxes of the social crisis, but rather reflected the fact that the Labour party had finished second in the 1920 elections, ahead of the Liberals, and that for fifteen years the traditional two-party system was replaced by a three-party society. The problem was one of adaptation of structures; the period from 1920 to

111

1935 was one of transition between the two-party system of the nine-teenth century (Conservatives and Liberals) and that of the twentieth (Labour in opposition to a Conservative party that represented a merger between the old Conservatives and the majority of the old Liberals; this resulted in a polarization of Socialists and Capitalists). During the fif-teen years of the three-party structure in Britain, the system functioned badly for technical reasons; the single-ballot majority vote, without runoffs, produced abnormal results when more than two parties were contesting.

In 1922, the Conservatives won 322 seats in the House of Commons —which represented a large majority—with 38.2 percent of the popular vote. In 1923, no party had a majority and Labour had to govern in concert with the Liberals. In 1929, the election results were even stranger; Labour won 287 seats with 8,362,000 votes, the Conservatives had 255 seats with 8,664,000 votes, and the Liberals took 58 seats with 5,300,000 votes. This resulted in the formation of the National Union government, a coalition of the Liberals and Conservatives under Ram-say MacDonald, which led to the temporary dislocation of the Labour party. Ultimately, the electoral machinery, which had been responsible for these parliamentary crises, itself provided a solution. The two-party structure having been reestablished in 1935, British governments re-gained their customary homogeneous, disciplined majorities. The insti-tutions were reinforced, though this did not prevent the governments from weakening in confrontations with the dictatorships, as illustrated by the lamentable policies of Neville Chamberlain.

The impotence of the liberal democracies in the 1930s in the face of the menace of Hitler was the product of the fundamental failure of their political institutions to adapt to a new society. The weak state of classic liberalism, the bargain-price state, the impotent state was not capable of dealing with the problems of the twentieth century. Govern-ments had to face problems that were not comparable in scope to those of the prewar years because of their geographical extension and their technical complexity. The famous "Eastern Question"—concerning the integrity of the Ottoman Empire and the position of Russia in Eastern Europe—the headache of turn-of-the-century diplomats, was a child's puzzle beside the reconstruction of Europe after 1918, the organization of a planned economy, control of currency, the development of inter-national trade. Hitler's government created a state apparatus suited to the new dimensions of new problems, while the liberal democracies clung to their old nineteenth-century instruments of government, patching them here and there. The superiority of the former over the latter derived not from its dictatorial but from its modern character. The competition between totalitarian and liberal systems in the 1930s was not unlike that between taxicabs and hansoms.

This aspect of the crisis in democratic institutions would not emerge into broad daylight until June 1940, when German dive-bombers brought to reality the old terror of the Gauls, who, according to Julius Caesar, feared only one thing: "that the sky might fall on their heads." But other, less dramatic symptoms had emerged during the preceding twenty years. Between 1920 and 1940 Western politicians were no worse than those of the preceding half-century. But they seemed more mediocre, more lackluster, more powerless because the world in which they worked had changed. With the exception of Franklin D. Roosevelt, they were no longer equal to the problems they faced. The solution did not lie in placing supermen at the head of states—as a general rule this is impossible. The structures of societies no longer allowed them to be governed by individuals: they had to be led by organizations, in politics as in economics. Individualist democracy had to give way to the technodemocracy that in fact supplanted it after 1945.

Part Three:
Technodemocracy
(1945-   )

In 1945, after twenty years of serious crisis, the Western system embarked on a new phase of growth. Political freedom regained its worth for Europeans, who had been stripped of it for four years, except in Britain, Sweden, and Switzerland. Crushed by fascism, they had seen its naked face: the Gestapo, the SS, torture, death camps, the genocide of the Jews. A certain prewar romanticism, that of Drieu la Rochelle and Brasillach,[1] which made fun of the sack-suited ordinary citizens of Paris and London and idealized the uniformed swaggerers of Rome and Berlin, shattered on impact with reality. By 1918, four years of trenches had given rise to a tremendous need for peace. In 1945, five years of totalitarian rule exploded in an irresistible demand for democracy.

Economic expansion followed liberation. From 1950 on, capitalism experienced a staggering growth in the advanced industrial nations. The landing of two men on the moon in 1969 was a symbol of the technical progress that transformed the worlds of production (automation), research and thought (computers), daily life (radio, television, transportation, accelerated city growth, and so on). The liberal economy seemed to have overcome its cyclical crises and to be subject to nothing worse than minor recessions. An inflationary tendency continued to grow, but as a rule it was held within acceptable limits. Thus, the Western nations were approaching a consumer society in which all man's essential needs could be satisfied—not only the primary ones (food, shelter, clothing, security) but also the secondary ones (comfort, leisure, culture). In other words, these nations were beginning to be free of the law of scarcity that had paralyzed earlier societies, under which there were never enough goods available to meet needs for them. Capitalism's material success was the more dazzling by reason of the coincident crisis of socialism in the Soviet Union and the European people's democracies, in which at first collective

---

1. French novelists who collaborated with the Germans after the defeat of France in 1940.—Translator.

*production and planning had brought about rapid, scientific
industrialization. The Communist model of development had
demonstrated its efficacity in breaking the chains of backward
economies. But the transition to a second phase, the stage that
would lead to a consumer society, proved to be much more arduous.
It required changes in structures that the Socialist countries did
not yet clearly recognize. Thus, they appeared to be marking time
in the 1960s.*

*Their economic problems were accompanied by a decline in
de-Stalinization. The passage from dictatorial to liberal communism
seemed even more difficult than that from the first to the second
phase of industrialization. As of now, Communist societies can
show no example that corresponds to the degree of economic and
political development achieved by the Western nations. It is not
inconceivable that a Communist society could achieve this level
of development, but none has yet done so. The Western system, which
combines undeniable economic efficiency with a substantial degree
of political freedom, is at present without a rival in the highly
developed societies.*

*Thus, the Western system has regained the firm roots that it had
lost in 1914, but at the cost of a profound transformation: liberal
democracy has given way to "technodemocracy." The former was
founded on economic competition and the law of the marketplace; the
latter is based on large enterprises with collective management,
which plan their activities and force the use of their products
through advertising and the mass media. The former preferred a weak
state that did not meddle in the economic realm; the latter
requires governments that impose broad regulation of production,
consumption, and trade by means of varying actions and incentives.
The former had to deal with weak, barely structured parties based
on leader groups, which gave political competition the character
of a gladiatorial combat; the latter confronts mass parties and
organizations, disciplines their leaders and followers, and marshals
them for collective action. Public administrations and private firms
resort to analogous structures. They become vast, complex,
hierarachical organizations.*

Technodemocracy and liberal democracy are alike in the unity of their economic and their political aspects. Both show a predominance of large organized entities in which decisions are usually made in the framework of a structured group that is itself linked to other groups. Technicians take part in these decisions, alongside the elected representatives of the people or the owners of capital. Such decisions are the consequence not so much of pressure from below—the voters, the customers—as of the desire to plot a future course defined at the top and made acceptable to the rank and file through propaganda and advertising. Some political and economic activities avoid this modern structure and retain their traditional character, but their importance is progressively diminishing.

Technodemocracy's material success has not fallen off in recent years. But since the student revolts of 1967 in the United States and Germany and especially the French students' rising in May 1968, the Western system has been under challenge by segments of the young and the intellectuals—a deeper and more violent challenge than it ever had to face in the worst of the repressions of the 1930s. No one can say whether this may have initiated a new crisis that will rock the system to its foundations or whether this agitation will confine itself to the very marginal circles in which it has so far appeared.

Chapter Seven

The New Oligarchy

The development of technodemocracy represented a transformation in the forces of production analogous to the Industrial Revolution of the nineteenth century, which had led to the spread of liberal democracy. At the same time, side by side with the classic inventions that had made it possible to master the forces of nature and increase the supply of consumer goods and services, there were major technological innovations: those, for example, that enhanced the powers of the human mind (computers) or the efficacy of influence over men (psychoanalysis). New technical advances accelerated the trend toward the establishment of huge collective organizations: giant enterprises, mass political parties, trade unions and powerful pressure groups, vast administrative entities, and so on. Production could reach its full development only with large-scale organizations and with a large market.

Thus, the economic oligarchy was transformed. No longer did it consist solely of the owners of the means of production and their straw men. Now it also included a broader social group comprising technicians, administrators, organizers, and middle management. Some observers, in fact, believe that capitalists have been thrust into a subordinate position and have lost control of the economy and politics, though this has not been proved. In any case, the new oligarchy is more closely bound than its predecessor to management and the state: it needs them more and it dominates them more effectively. Furthermore, the large-scale production that is characteristic of highly industrialized societies cannot evolve within national limits, which become too confining. The economic oligarchy tends to become multinational, and this, from another point of view, raises the problem of its relations with the political arm.

The Structure of the New Oligarchy

The oligarchy that controlled liberal democracy was composed of capitalists—owners of the means of production. Technicians, administrators, politicians could become part of this oligarchy (as, earlier, commoners had been able to rise to the nobility), but they played only a secondary part in it, unless they were absorbed into their new environment and became capitalists in their turn. Moreover, by no means all businessmen became part of the oligarchy, which admitted only the most important. Small individual enterprisers (farmers, artisans, merchants) were excluded, though on the whole they supported its actions. It endeavored, too, to create a solidarity—or a pseudo-solidarity—with them to maintain their allegiance.

The oligarchy that manages technodemocracy does not have the same structure. One can challenge the statement of contemporary Western writers that capitalists are excluded from it. But it is undeniable that technicians, managers, and scientists now form an increasingly large proportion of it and hold a more important position. Even if they have not taken over all power, they now possess a good share of it. What is more, the oligarchy has refined its ties with the state and its means of dominating the citizenry. The development of the mass media allows a much more thorough conditioning by means of advertising and propaganda, which creates a consensus that, in spite of its artificial quality, is broader and deeper.

The "Technostructure"

For a quarter of a century, Western economists and sociologists have supposed that the economic oligarchy changed character within contemporary neocapitalism. In 1948, in his book *Managerial Revolution*, James Burnham described the revolution of the "managers" or "organizers" who had taken over control of private firms from the capitalists. Others saw the technicians as the successors to the owners of the means of production; a whole literature developed around "technocracy." In 1967, John Kenneth Galbraith undertook a more systematic and deeper study of contemporary great industries. He described their collective management, which brought together everyone who had information necessary to the firm's operation, and he baptized it "technostructure."

This description may be used as a point of departure for an analysis of the new oligarchy. To Galbraith the nature of the technostructure lay in the collective character of its decisions. Thus he was in diametrical opposition to Koestler, who merely supplanted the individual capitalist entrepreneur with a technocratic one. In reality, large industrial firms can only be managed collectively, because management requires a collection of complex data dealing with production methods, problems of projection and planning, the social organization of the company, its financing, marketing, and so on. No one person alone can assimilate the sum of these data; hence, it is necessary to bring various specialists together in a group to arrive at decisions—the sole means of evaluating the pertinence of each individual element; the degree of credence that can be given to it; and, consequently, the chances of the firm's progress. It is all of these specialists that constitute the technocracy.

To Galbraith, the capitalist is not a member of the decision-making group. General meetings of stockholders are only receptacles for reports prepared by the technostructure. The owners do not meddle with it as long as it provides them with a reasonable profit. The existence of this profit is a condition of the enterprise's operation, but it no longer represents the prime motive. It is rather a charge on the business, like taxes, social security, or interest on loans; consequently, shares of stocks become somewhat like bonds. The expansion of the firm has ousted profit as the essential objective that affords the basic economic momentum. It is growth that counts and on which the members of the managing class depend for the enhancement of their material advantages and the broadening of their power. Personal gain remains the basic wellspring of economic activity, in accord with liberal theories; but it is no longer confused with profit.

These mechanisms, however, are not universally applicable to production. Galbraith distinguishes between two sectors, or "subsystems," in the Western industrial nations. Below a certain minimum size, it is no longer possible for a company to assemble sufficient capital for the construction of factories and for their survival during the long gestation period that lies between the decision to produce and the placement of the product on the market, and for the protection of the firm against possible fluctuations in prices, costs, or customer preferences. There is, on the other hand, no upper limit on size. There is good reason to believe that the larger an industrial company becomes, the more efficient it becomes. This is the reason that industrial firms tend to become gigantic.

In contrast to the first sector—the huge firms organized on the basis of "technostructure"—the small and medium-sized enterprises constitute the second economic sector, keeping alive a traditional capitalism more or less modified by state controls. Galbraith reckons that in the United States both subsystems are of virtually equal importance: some two thousand corporations engaging in transportation, power production, communications, distribution, and public services provide 40 percent of the Gross National Product, as do the ten million farmers, artisans, small retailers, individual suppliers of services, artists, and so on. In other, less advanced Western countries, the technostructure sector is probably less important, even though it embraces nationalized enterprises. In any event, it holds the upper hand because it provides the direction for the whole; its managing class, therefore, constitutes the core of the economic oligarchy.

As Galbraith describes it, the new oligarchy is no longer based on the inheritance of ownership of property, which succeeded the inheritance of titles of nobility when capitalism came into being. It is based rather on the co-optation, by the members of the technostructure, of those whose knowledge and skills are necessary to the enterprise. Thus, the ruling oligarchy is more mobile, less certain of the morrow, and at the same time more open and more democratic. The chances of admission for noncapitalists is greater, provided that they have the necessary intellectual and technical qualifications. Meritocracy takes the place of plutocracy, establishing a different kind of rivalry in place of the competition of classic liberalism.

Galbraith's analysis is the best of all those offered by neoliberals in explanation of the structure of Western industry and of the economic oligarchy. Nonetheless, it is not without some errors or basic gaps. In the first place, it underestimates the function of the capitalists. Galbraith opens the door for his critics when he says that the technostructure's power is "absolute as long as the firm produces a minimum of profit." Thus, that power becomes relative when this "minimum of profit" is not achieved. Then the stockholders exercise their rights again; they can freely eliminate the members of the technostructure and replace them with others. The fact that the king allows his chief minister to govern while things are going well (as Louis XIII of France did with Richelieu), or even that he allows the minister to choose his own successor (as Richelieu designated Mazarin), does not mean the elimination of power of the throne, which, on the contrary, retains a supreme, sovereign quality. In a certain sense, the capitalist possesses an analogous power over the technostructure.

Not every capitalist possesses this power, obviously; the mass of small stockholders is, as a rule, powerless. While some chance agitator may succeed in mobilizing it, this occurs extremely seldom and never has any sequel. But Galbraith does not adequately distinguish between this mass and the few big stockholders who, in fact, control stockholders' meetings and who are less and less often individuals and more and more frequently organizations. The "two hundred families" whom the French Popular Front attacked in 1936, and whose members domi-nated the whole economy through the corporations of which they were stockholders, represented a transition stage between liberal capitalism and contemporary neocapitalism, like the barons of American industry a few decades earlier. Today, corporate shares are owned by commer-cial banks, credit corporations, huge firms, and holding companies, which in this fashion pretty much control the majority of the big corporations.

Private ownership of the means of production, having passed from individual enterprisers to industrial and commercial corporations, is now in the hands of financial groups that own a sufficient share of an organization's capital to give them control of its management. In addi-tion, they assume various guises. Some have a nucleus composed of a huge firm that more or less directly controls other enterprises through agreements, mergers, subsidiaries, holding arrangements, and so on. Others, such as commercial banks or credit companies, engage more or less exclusively in financial operations. A distinction between the two categories is often difficult—whether, for instance, a commercial bank controls or is controlled by a giant industrial firm. In any event, the collective nature of the ownership of stock in the corporations con-trolled does not eliminate its capitalist character, nor does the fact that the financial firms, too, are managed by a technostructure in which experts, specialists, and administrators take part in decisions alongside the big stockholders who hold the supreme power.

Galbraith commits another error. Not only does he minimize the part played by the capitalist in the technostructure, in which the capitalist has the final word; he also considers only the technostructure as it exists within the framework of the individual enterprise. The technostructures at this first level are coordinated and organized at a second level by a kind of superior technostructure composed of the managing directors of the giant corporations, the holding companies, the financial corporations, and the commercial banks that control most of the large enterprises. There is even a third level, composed of the chief stockholders of a group of giant enterprises—holding companies, financial corporations, and commercial banks—as well as their experts, counselors, and administrators. This supreme technostructure is the analogue, in the oligarchy of neocapitalism, to the princes of the blood in the old aristocracy.

Such a description is at once a flight of fantasy and a genuine analysis of the evolution in economic structures. It is fantasy because the interplay of different groups at different levels conceals the fact that there are a few men who control a vast number of boards of directors. In legal terms, the two hundred families no longer exist. In practical terms, they can be found in virtually every strategic center—banks, holding companies, finance corporations, large firms—from which the modern economy is ruled. But the substitution of collective dukedoms for individual baronies is intended to do more than mask the power of capitalists. It also modifies the modes by which that power is exercised, and this constitutes a real transformation of the Western system.

The technostructure does not eliminate the power of the owners of the means of production and substitute the power of the technicians, experts, scientists, and organizers who take part in collective decisions. By bringing both groups together, it makes it possible for the capitalists to have access to the whole of the data necessary for knowledgeable management. At the corporate level, the capitalists generally are content to hand over power to the specialist group that constitutes the technostructure as long as things go well, reclaiming that power as soon as things go badly. In the world of commercial banks, financial corporations, huge firms, and holding companies, the capitalists work more closely with the collective management, and the function of the experts is rather that of advisers, like the relation of the clergy and the lawyers to the feudal kings and lords.

Another characteristic of the new economic oligarchy ought not to be forgotten: the very scope of large firms, the need to expand their markets and their sources of raw materials, the conditions under which new inventions can be exploited—all of these things drive them to transcend the boundaries of nations. The operation of participation creates a tendency toward a multinational oligarchy. But the inequalities among the nations involved, one of which is much larger than the others, usually cause the multinationality to be more apparent than real, so that it ends by being dominated by the United States. To the extent to which the economic oligarchy shapes politics, this tends toward aligning the West on Washington. We will return to this problem presently.

The New Oligarchy and the State

The new oligarchy is far more dependent than the old on the state. What the old oligarchy wanted more than anything was that the state should do nothing. Neocapitalism, in contrast, requires a strong, active state, capable of regulating the operation of the economy and maintaining the conditions necessary to growth. Previously, production was governed by the laws of the marketplace; depending on buyers' preferences, one enterprise flourished while another declined. Technical advances were based on individual inventions that were put to the test of competition by enterprisers. Today, large industries' manufacturing programs are settled several years before the product can be offered for sale. In part, these programs follow consumer choices as revealed by market research. But, once the programs have been set in motion, these choices must be prevented from changing; in fact, they must be reinforced through advertising campaigns. Consumers' purchasing power, too, must be sustained, if not increased, and this presupposes an overall coordination of the economy.

It is no longer possible to guarantee such coordination by liberal methods. The elimination of the less efficient businesses by the more efficient is no longer tolerable when it is a question of giant organizations whose disappearance would throw thousands of wage-earners out of work. Nor is it any longer a factor when consumer preferences are conditioned by advertising campaigns. The instruments of competition can no longer establish the worth of rival innovations, which now require huge investments without any assurance of profitability in either the short or the long term. Research, too, assumes new dimensions. Technical progress is now much more dependent on the state than on private ingenuity. Even the gigantic American aircraft firms need public funds to develop their new models. Without such funds, neither the jet engine nor the discovery of atomic energy would have been possible. Government intervention has to expand beyond the narrow sense of the word and include the basic investments necessary to the initiation of industrial production.

The state is equally necessary to the development of the nonprofit infrastructures and public services. Capitalist firms, by definition, cannot undertake these tasks. But they find it more and more necessary that the public authorities do so, because these infrastructures and services are indispensable to their activities. In a more general way, they need state regulation of the economy as a whole, stimulating consumption when the danger of recession appears and restraining it when inflationary pressure becomes too great. Liberal institutions had never wholly guaranteed this total equilibrium, because they were unable to prevent cyclical crises, though they could confine them within certain limits when the economy was founded on real competition among a host of small and medium firms. As early as the 1930s, it was common knowledge that these liberal institutions were paralyzed in the face of production by large entities, a situation which had already come into being in the United States and Germany. Today, no one any longer questions the necessity for action by the public authorities.

Such intervention cannot be contained within national borders. It has to develop on the international level as well, in order to guarantee foreign markets and the acquisition of raw materials. This was already being done in the liberal democracies, but now it has assumed a new breadth. The huge industrial enterprises are of a size that precludes their developing only within national limits. No longer does their foreign expansion depend only on their ability to compete; it derives rather from agreements made between governments in a world in which economic borders have never been wholly opened and have often been closed. Hence, industry unconditionally needs the support of the state, which alone can make possible the international growth that industry requires.

In industrial nations, this support takes the form of agreements negotiated on a basis of relative equality. In the relations between the West and the Third World, it generally assumes an imperialist character. This was already apparent under liberal democracy, which accomplished the great colonial conquests of 1890-1914. But at that time, imperialism was marginal. Today the situation has changed. Not only does the size of the major Western enterprises require that foreign markets be available to them but, above all, the collective economy of the industrial nations needs the raw materials of the Third World if it is to survive. Therefore, imperialism is no longer a subsidiary but an essential activity in the developed nations, necessary to the maintenance and expansion of their scale of living.

It assumes new forms because of the nationalist drive in the Third World that has liberated the classic colonies, which are now independent states. They are subjected to an economic neocolonialism based on the inequality of exchanges between the industrial countries and the developing nations. In certain instances, this neocolonialism is practiced directly by private firms from industrial countries without help from their public authorities. In others, governments help their industries become established or protect them against nationalization. Whether it consists of military action, the organization of local conspiracies, or trade negotiations, the state's intervention is equally important.

Because the economic oligarchy's need of the state has increased, its need to control the state rigorously has become more urgent. In a liberal democracy, it was possible to envisage that public power might come into the hands of men independent of the lords of industry and trade; if they restricted themselves to assuring domestic tranquillity and foreign protection, the market economy could progress satisfactorily. Under technodemocracy, such liberty for the state in relation to business is absolutely unthinkable, for business is very substantially dependent on the decisions made by the state. The new oligarchy knows that more than ever it has to maintain its control over the intermediate class that wields political power.

But that oligarchy still relies on traditional means. The corruption of politicians or officials at the national level plays an increasingly marginal part. It makes it possible merely to maintain a few trusted agents (who are generally being watched) at strategic points. At the same time, such corruption persists to a greater degree at the local level: collusion between city governments and highway-construction firms or building contractors is typical. The financing of election campaigns is still important, especially since their cost has risen with the growth of the means of communication. It is essential that these always be controlled by the economic oligarchy. This control is not substantially infringed by the appearance of independent newspapers financed by trade unions or mass parties, because they are compelled to "depoliticize" to reach a big audience within the cultural structure imposed by the oligarchy. The state's monopoly of radio and television could give it great freedom of action; but, even where the state has this monopoly, it is seldom used because of the dependence of the state on the oligarchy.

Industrial, commercial, and agricultural pressure groups are still powerful and are usually dominated by the oligarchy. The conflict of interests between the advanced industrial sector and the traditional sector, however, occasionally incites flashes of independence in one or another group of small producers. Thus, a certain radicalization among small farmers and retailers has emerged since 1950 in western Europe. In recent years, the parties of the left have attempted to exploit it; in certain cases—for instance, the poor peasants in France—the Communists have partly succeeded. Such phenomena are peripheral, and the oligarchy retains its overall control of the capitalist pressure groups that help it dominate the state.

The growth of the economy endows it with new means of action in other ways. Galbraith has ably described the interrelations that have grown up in the United States between private enterprises and major governmental agencies, particularly the Army and NASA, in connection with state purchases. These orders guarantee the survival and expansion of some firms that could not stay alive without them. They represent a substantial part of the business of certain others. The growth of techno-structure within industrial firms is helpful to their collaboration with public bodies. In both, in fact, the experts, the technicians, and the scientists participate in decisions in the same way. Since they have the same training and speak the same language, they find it easy to understand each other.

They also share the same interests: technicians, whether private or public, are equally eager to increase their power, thus enhancing their prestige and sometimes their incomes. Prestige becomes what counts most beyond a certain level of income and social position. NASA and the firms that work for it share a common interest in fostering the expansion of the space program; the Air Force and the aircraft makers have the same interest in a greater emphasis on fighter planes and bombers rather than on submarines, and so on. Thus, a symbiosis develops between firms and governmental units that together constitute new pressure groups endowed with considerable power. With the United States Army's $60 billion of orders a year, the "military-industrial complex," of which Eisenhower spoke in a moment of insight, represents the world's most highly developed planned sector.

The interlocking of private firms and public agencies has not reached so great a concentration in the other Western nations. But it is developing among them in similar forms. In France, between 1919 and 1929, government technicians moved over into private industry. Although there has been substantial increase in the phenomenon since 1945, it is still marginal. Regular relations and reciprocal ties between private and public technostructures are far more important. They tend to align the public on the private, because the private technostructures have a dominant position in the French economy. For the same reason, nationalized enterprises tend at times to align themselves on capitalist firms. This reinforces the oligarchy's grip on the state, rather than weakening it.

Beyond these specific means of pressure, whether traditional or new, the oligarchy's control of the state is based on the fact that both now share the same fundamental objective, economic expansion. Growth tends to become the major myth of all Western societies. Unquestionably, it amounts to more than a myth, since improvement in the scale of community living depends on it. But the theme of growth goes beyond these material advances: it represents the supreme goal of human societies. A recession is not only a temporary material impoverishment but a defeat, a setback, engendering frustrations and complexes.

Did the oligarchy deliberately inspire this myth with the help of the mass media that it controls to reinforce its power, or did the myth arise spontaneously out of the materialism of industrial societies and their belief in progress? It makes little difference. The power of the myth compels politicians to present their electors with economic success. To a certain extent, this success depends on the politicians, because they still exert some influence over production. But it depends even more on the great private firms—in other words, the oligarchy. In the cooperation between them and the state their weight is greater and so is their influence in joint decisions.

The economic oligarchy's power is enhanced by its concentration. Its

128

numbers are gradually diminished, until it includes only the managers of the great industrial and financial corporations, who are constantly decreasing in number and increasing in strength. True, the state also represents a concentration because of the strengthening of the executive, the evolution of presidential power, and, in particular, the growth of rigid political parties that can guarantee disciplined majorities. But the range of the two phenomena is not comparable. The concentration of economic power is stronger and swifter than that of political power, which, therefore, is less capable of opposition to the economic. This is all the more the case in that the industrial and financial oligarchy is more stable than that of the politicians, whose reelection is never certain, in spite of the rigid parties and precisely because of their pluralism.

The state's dependency in comparison with that of the economic oligarchy is, therefore, greater in modern technodemocracy than it was in the liberal democracy of 1870-1939. But the problem of this dependency is posed in qualitative rather than quantitative terms, in direct proportion to the changes in the character of the oligarchy effected by the development of multinational firms. Besides, the word "multinational" more often than not disguises a participation by American capital in European enterprises that is almost always the majority share, or at least very large. The size and power of American firms usually guarantee their domination of the other nationalities. As a result, control of the political power by the economic oligarchy becomes the control of a national power by a partly foreign oligarchy in which the alien component is very strong. This is how American economic power colonizes the other Western nations.

The creation of a European political community seems incapable of averting this development. The distribution of jurisdictions among national governments and a federal authority would further weaken the individual nations in their dealings with the multinational oligarchy. The federal body could have no very great powers until and unless there develops among the European countries a far closer and stronger solidarity than that existing within any individual nation. One may well doubt whether such a condition can be met for many decades. In any case, even a strong federal government like that of the United States is controlled by the economic oligarchy; it is impossible to imagine how a European government could escape this control. Furthermore, the exis tence or nonexistence of a political community can hardly influence European firms' decisions to open their doors to American participation. These decisions are based on economic motives quite independent of nationalism or federalism.

The development of multinational firms under American dominance and their influence on European states cannot be prevented within the capitalist framework. The expansion of European enterprises and their extension beyond national frontiers are required by the conditions of modern production. It is to their interest to profit by the advances made by the United States in the spheres of technique, organization, and commercialization. This kind of interest remains the basic motivation of private firms. In this domain, the state cannot stand against their decisions. There is no benefit to it in so doing, for then American investments would go to neighboring nations. A Europe-wide regimentation might restrict this development to a degree, but it could not stop or even retard it, for it is the expression of pressures that are too strong to be overcome. The development of technodemocracy in the direction of semicolonization of the West by the United States appears to be inevitable.

Controlling the Masses

The fact that the economic oligarchy dominates the politicians and the administrators who manage the machinery of the states would be of no great significance if the oligarchy did not control, at the same time, the masses of the people that elect and dismiss those members of the intermediate class through the workings of universal suffrage. Such control is never absolute, but it is always very tight. Technodemocracy, like liberal democracy, commingles the influence of the masses with the influence of money. The mixture varies from nation to nation both in its proportions and in its modalities. In certain respects, the control of the masses is more difficult today for the oligarchy; in other respects, it is easier. New methods arise side by side with traditional methods, and the whole of social life is profoundly changed by them.

The Development of Consensus

Several of the characteristics of technodemocracy make control of the masses more difficult for it than for liberal democracy. First of all, limitations on voting rights have virtually disappeared. Income, property, and tax qualifications no longer exist. In the United States, the Supreme Court has outlawed poll taxes and literacy requirements, which made it possible to prevent the blacks from voting; similar curbs elsewhere had long since disappeared. The upper houses of legislatures were abolished in Denmark in 1953 and in Sweden in 1968; in other countries, the influence of the upper chamber is usually weak and its membership is chosen much like that of the lower chamber, with a tendency toward diminution in inequalities of representation. In the United States Senate, however, inequality has been preserved because of federalism: the preponderance of less populated states—which are often the most conservative—is still overwhelming. Inequalities are increasingly sharp in the French Senate because of urbanization; but the Senate today can hardly oppose the decisions of the National Assembly—the new name for the lower house of the parliament, previously called the Chamber of Deputies. Hence, the oligarchy is obliged to adjust to universal suffrage, which now operates throughout the West.

Except in the United States, the evolution of mass parties and labor organizations more or less closely bound to them assures the citizenry of more effective means of actions as a counterbalance to the influence of money than those available under liberal democracy. Dues and assessments levied on their members now provide parties and unions with substantial war chests. These funds also support newspapers that are independent of financiers and that constitute important instruments for propaganda. They are, as it were, strong points impervious to the influence of the economic oligarchy and theoretically capable of serving as a counterweight to it. Obviously, they are more effective when they reject the political influence of capitalism, as the Socialists and Communists do. Even the conservative mass parties—Liberals or Christian Democrats—which tolerate capitalism more easily, retain nevertheless an autonomous power, by reason of their structures and their numbers. It is on these that their leaders depend to resist pressures from the oligarchy.

The decline of religion also weakened the oligarchy's hold over the masses. In Catholic countries, the alliance between throne and altar had been succeeded by that between capital and altar at the end of the nineteenth century. This latter alliance contributed substantially to the maintenance of the existing order, based on private ownership of the means of production. It compelled Christians to respect private property and the authority of its owners. In Protestant countries, the alliance was less formal because of the lack of any ecclesiastical centralization, but sometimes it was deeper as a result of the Calvinist and Puritan concepts that sanctified economic success. The emphasis on sexual morality at the expense of community morality was favorable to capitalism. The weakening of religious belief deprived capitalism of the support of the churches. Because this deterioration was less marked in the United States than elsewhere, the American oligarchy was better able to retain support from the churches. But while traditional Christianity was declining, a new type of Christianity was, as we shall see, being reborn in small groups, where it became a more intense and more genuine way of life.

Other elements of technodemocracy, in contrast, facilitate the oligarchy's control over the popular masses. All these are more or less based on the growth of social consensus and the diminution of the class struggle. Liberal democracy was able to expand when the conflict between the aristocracy and the middle classes had slackened enough to allow them to live side by side in peace. In addition, because of the Socialists' weakness, their isolation, and the lack of credibility of their doctrines, the strife between capitalists and proletarians did not seem intense enough (in spite of its violence) to destroy the established order. After 1917, when the accession of communism in the Soviet Union had revived Socialist hopes, made their doctrines more believable, and spurred fear of the "Reds" in the middle classes, the class struggle became sharper and democratic institutions went through a crisis. The new vigor of these institutions after 1945 coincided with the assimilation of socialism into the Western system—there was a new decline in the class struggle and a fresh infusion of consensus about the system.

At first glance, this state of affairs seemed to have been born of the unanimous devotion of all citizens of the West to political freedoms. That these were limited, and restricted particularly by capitalism's power and its control over the machinery of the state, was quite generally agreed. But it was also quite generally believed that limited freedoms were better than no freedoms at all. The war had given great impetus to this belief by placing millions of Europeans under dictatorship for a number of years and laying bare the horrors of nazism. The governments of Eastern Europe had fortified the feeling that the West's freedoms represented a fundamental good, in spite of the defects of capitalism.

The Socialist parties drew the logical conclusions from these facts. In practice they all became reformist after 1945. Some, indeed, abandoned the notion of instituting socialism and confined themselves to modifying capitalism to make it more favorable to the workers. As for the others, their references to socialism seemed more ritual than real, at least between 1950 and 1960. But thereafter anticapitalism came back to life. There was general agreement on a liberal, pluralistic, and democratic socialism. Even the Western Communist parties began to concede the value of political freedoms and to include them in their plans for the new society. Today they proclaim that they will gain power through legal elections and that political pluralism will be preserved during the period of building socialism and in the Socialist state.

But their definition of this pluralism is not yet firm. However, even if western Communists' support of political liberalism was a Machiavellian trick, it would, nevertheless, attest to the fact that their voters and their militants were attached to freedom, inasmuch as the party had had to satisfy them on this point. This means support for neocapitalism, since there currently exists no model of liberal socialism, but only experiments in dictatorial socialism. Lacking such a model, many in the West resigned themselves to freedom without socialism, because they refused to sacrifice freedom for socialism.

This attitude owed something, too, to the evolution of capitalism, which itself had incorporated certain elements of socialism. The substitution of the "welfare state" for the classic liberal state had not brought total well-being to the workers—far from it; but it had considerably reduced their miseries. In Europe, they were protected by a social-security system against the possibilities of accident, illness, motherhood, permanent disability, and old age. There were serious gaps in this system because of the flaws in public health, the inadequacy of old-age pensions, the persistence of unsecured employment; but certain capitalist countries governed by Social Democrats had learned to fill the gaps quite admirably—Sweden was an example—and this fed the hope of similar improvements elsewhere. State action was often insufficient in the areas of controlling prices, supporting purchasing power, regulating the economy, providing for the retraining of workers in obsolete

133

sectors, assisting weakened enterprises, developing public services and collective amenities, and broadening free schooling. Nonetheless, it demonstrated the possibility of expanding such action in all these domains.

Is it necessary to point out that the very path taken by neocapitalism corresponded in part to the conceptions put forth by the Social Democrats between 1919 and 1939? The control of credit and currency, the regulation of economic activity, the development of a public and a semipublic sector, collective bargaining, labor unions, cooperation in planning and economic direction, worker participation in management—all these things were more or less embryonic in the ideas evolved by the Socialist parties between the two world wars. Capitalism is able to survive today only because of the aspects of socialism that it contains. It is natural that Socialists should accept this mixed system more easily than the purely liberal one that prevailed before. Western capitalism has moved in their direction; hence their support.

Without doubt, this development of capitalism is still something of an illusion. It has been accused of socializing its losses. The economic oligarchy is glad to work for the nationalization of unprofitable sectors, which then can provide private enterprises with cheap products and services and enable them to increase their profits at the expense of the taxpayers. There are innumerable examples of the sort, some traditional (public transport, electric power) and others new (public reclamation of lands subsequently turned over to private promoters; state financing of research, the results of which are exploited by private industry). In other spheres, the socialization of capitalism is more real, particularly in social security and public services, which are essential to the entire citizenry.

Capitalism's material successes probably have still more influence on the growth of a general consensus. Studies have shown that workers are especially sensitive to the level of real wages, which govern their standard of living. In this domain, technodemocracy has made enormous progress since 1945. It has not reached the threshold of a consumer society; even in the richest countries, such as the United States, a large part of the population endures major deprivation. But the great majority lives increasingly better, or at least less badly. Income rises, and with it material comfort (television sets, household appliances, variety in clothing, leisure, vacations). The situation of the mass of the people is not much to be envied, given the problems of city life, daily commuting, housing, employment; but the situation has become more tolerable. Above all, it is improving fairly regularly, as is shown by the growth in purchasing power.

It will be objected that this growth is more illusory than real, because needs (more or less artificially created by advertising) increase even more rapidly. Thus, there is a growing gap between demand and capacity to buy; in the last analysis, there is mounting pauperization rather than growth in income. There is some truth to this analysis. But it would seem that new needs, as a rule, are less strongly felt than basic needs, and the impression of a rise in income is still very widely experienced. In any event, the citizens of present-day Western societies believe that they would not enjoy a higher scale of life under other systems. The economic semifailure of the Soviet Union and the people's democracies has heightened the adverse reaction created by their political authoritarianism. The idea is growing that though capitalism may not be satisfactory, socialism, in its current form, is even less so. Obviously, this idea fosters assimilation into technodemocracy.

The fact that modes of living are becoming more homogeneous exerts pressure in the same direction. Granted that the range of real incomes in Western societies is very broad and that ways of living are most varied. Nonetheless, if one leaves aside, on the one hand, a group of leaders and notables (including the economic oligarchs, prominent figures in the arts and the mass media, outstanding physicians and lawyers, and so on) and, on the other hand, the poor (the blacks, immigrant workers, and so on), the rest—that is, the great majority of the population—is divided into only two broad categories. The cadres, in the broad sense of the term, constitute an upper middle class. This class includes technicians, experts, and directors of private firms, administrators in the public sector, jurists, university teachers, and so forth. Clerical and factory workers, small shopkeepers, artisans, farmers, and so on, represent a lower middle class. Within each group, modes of living are rather alike. Although there are differences between the groups, they tend to converge. Films, radio, television, and the popular press foster a culture that is favorable to this process.

It is undeniable that the homogeneity of modes of living is more apparent than real and that it conceals great disparities in job problems, relations with the employer, job security, and income levels. The fact

135

remains, however, that social barriers have been lowered in the industrial societies and that some categories, such as factory workers and peasants, are no longer, or are much less, isolated from the rest of the population. In other words, they are better integrated into the community. Trade-union and political traditions have curbed this evolution in Europe, but they have been unable to eliminate its effects completely. Similarities in ways of living and the consumption of the same mass-produced goods do not prevent conflicts of interest or of class, but they do mitigate them. More precisely, they lead them to develop within a single social framework, which is that of technodemocracy.

New Means of Control

The evolution of social consensus makes it easier for the economic oligarchy to control the masses of the people. Domination by the oligarchy is part of a system regarded, on the whole, as inevitable, even if some of its aspects are rejected. For many Europeans and for some Americans, the power of money is an unwelcome liability, which is tolerated for the ultimate profit to be derived. Even when efforts are made to restrain it, its existence is accepted simply because no other course is possible. But this resignation would not be enough if it were not reinforced by various factors that move the citizenry in the direction desired by the economic rulers. In this area, technodemocracy provides the oligarchy with new and highly efficacious weapons that supplement its traditional arms.

Traditional fear of the "Reds" was of great value during the cold war of the 1950s. In Europe, the Communists were isolated from the rest of the nation and thrust into a ghetto. This was the era when Guy Mollet, the Socialist, said of the Communists in France: "They are not on the left, they are in the east." In the United States, McCarthyism created an atmosphere of witch-hunting in universities and the government. Thus, opposition to the economic oligarchy was paralyzed. With the "thaw" and peaceful coexistence, such methods became more difficult to use. But the rebellion among the young and the students made it possible to have fresh recourse to them fifteen years later. The events of May 1968 in Paris assured the election of conservatives kindly disposed toward business. The activities of the leftists in the United States, France, and other countries helped mobilize the "silent majority"—the flock of bleating sheep that loyally follows the oligarchy's shepherds.

The forces of repression always rely on anti-Communist propaganda when the need arises. The conviction of Ethel and Julius Rosenberg in the United States matched that of Sacco and Vanzetti thirty years earlier. The police methods of Jules Moch, the French minister of the interior, were a continuation of those employed by his predecessors in the Third Republic and an omen of those of his successor in the Fifth. Leftists accused capitalist society of being "repressive." It was neither more nor less so than the societies that had gone before it in history; in truth, rather less. Every system, every state defends itself against the enemies who seek to overthrow it: the democratic system and the liberal state have done so with somewhat less violence, with somewhat more scruple, ever since they were relatively reassured by the crushing of the Paris Commune in 1871. The evolution of social consensus made it possible for technodemocracy to be even more gentle, once freed of the fear of communism of the 1950s. The activism of leftist groups is driving it once more to severity.

However, these classic means of controlling the people take second place to the new instruments of the mass media. Now, the national press, the radio, the movies, and especially television have a controlling influence in industrialized societies. They cannot, of course, impose any kind of idea or any kind of product, for they must take into account up to a certain point the beliefs of the citizens and the tastes of the consumers. But they have a wide margin of freedom. Opinions, habits, and behavior are deeply influenced by them in every respect: political, economic, literary, artistic, religious, sentimental, sexual. The control of the mass media is one of the basic sources of power in the industrialized societies.

In technodemocracies this control is exercised primarily by the economic oligarchy, either directly or indirectly. Some newspapers may escape control, as has been noted, either because they are cooperatively held by those who work for them or because they are supported by mass organizations, such as trade unions or political parties. They are the exception. But they must themselves take into account the general climate of opinion created by the mass media. They cannot afford to do away with the advertising that is necessary to cover some of their expenses but that limits their freedom. On all the other media the control of the oligarchy is greater. Radio and private television stations depend on the advertising of large companies—the only ones that have adequate financial means. In turn "public" radio and television networks are directed by administrators and men who themselves depend on the economic oligarchy, for reasons already discussed. Even institutions that appear to be independent, like the BBC, have rather limited freedom of action.

The economic structure of the technodemocracy makes control of the mass media by the oligarchy absolutely necessary. Industrial production no longer depends on the laws of the market and on the free choice of the buyers. Production plans are made long before the product reaches the market. Once a plan is made, the product must remain on the market for a period that is long enough to bring a return and cover investments. This period cannot be sustained without the help of large publicity firms and a long advertising campaign to convince the consumer to buy—that is, without the mass media. If radio, television, and the press were to stop advertising, the sale of many products would decline and a serious crisis would ensue.

The whole of the capitalist economy is based in the last analysis on the conditioning of men and women to buy. Of course, before a product comes to the market there are market studies to examine and study the desires of the consumers: there is no wholly artificial creation of needs by advertising campaigns. But without publicity the wants of the citizens would appear less urgent, less specific, and more diffuse. The machinery of fashion makes it possible to devaluate a product soon after the consumer has bought it. A similar product, say, a new "model" of a car, differing only slightly from its predecessor, is offered, and people buy it, for fear of seeming out of date or out of fashion if they do not. This process is required by the modern conditions of industry. To sell cheaply one must produce in great bulk; to produce in great quantity one must have a constant mass of buyers; to accomplish this one must make people disgusted or disenchanted as quickly as possible with the product they have already bought.

Fashion is one of the driving forces of contemporary capitalism. It is inseparable from mass advertising, which becomes both repressive and obsessive. Nothing is sillier than the praise of "experts" for the new fashion designers—for their creativity, spontaneity, their knowledge of the "modern woman," and so on. In reality all they try to do is to make last years designs "old" and incite everybody to buy what is "new." Complete renewal may be difficult to achieve. Hence there appears a certain balance between "daring" (which makes it obligatory to buy what is new) and "moderation" (which makes it possible to rework last year's things). The economic oligarchy has accomplished through advertising what dictatorships achieved through propaganda: to induce the public to buy products or ideas that were not particularly attractive initially but that were made familiar and acceptable through the media.

In politics, as well, large-scale use of the mass media has enabled the oligarchy to maintain an artificial consensus. Analysis of the television programs, the radio broadcasts, and the press of the Western democracies shows how constantly the following themes are repeated: the superiority of capitalist production, the dangers of socialism, the need for the concentration of firms, the skills of businessmen, the relative incompetence of the politicians, the inefficiency and high cost of public services, the dangers of opposing ideologies (that is, of efforts to envisage a society that is different from the existing one), and the irresponsible character of the intellectuals, who are portrayed as capable only of criticizing the established order.

Chapter Eight

The New Political Organization

Technodemocracy has preserved the institutional framework of liberal democracy. The new constitutions adopted in the countries liberated from fascism—Italy and Germany—were patterned on the traditional model. But technodemocracy has perfected a relatively new institution, which first appeared in some of the parliamentary governments set up between 1918 and 1920: the constitutional court. It proved to be an excellent weapon for the protection of civil liberties. It was not until 1962 that France adopted a political system of a semipresidential type; it had already existed in Finland, Austria, Iceland, and Weimar Germany. The election reforms of 1945 spread proportional representation throughout western Europe, extending the movement that had begun in 1900 and was further developed in 1918. Subsequently, the French went back to the old two-ballot majority system of the Third Republic (1958). Even the elimination of an upper chamber in Denmark (1953) and Sweden (1969) was a continuation of an earlier trend; Norway and Finland already had unicameral legislatures, and the decline of bicameralism was an almost universal phenomenon in the West, apart from nations having federal political systems.

Behind the traditional appearances thus kept alive, political organization was, in actuality, fundamentally transformed. The spread of rigid parties turned a democracy of individuals into a democracy of organizations. The United States and Japan remained outside the influence of this process, but they shared in the weakening of parliaments and the growth of the executive: this transfer of powers manifested itself everywhere, in most instances without constitutional reforms, simply through natural development. Neither of these trends was absolutely new. They had been observed between 1919 and 1939; in many countries, they had begun even earlier. After 1945, they assumed a new dimension; thereafter, they dominated the structure of Western political systems, which have since borne hardly any resemblance to the classic liberal model.

General Characteristics of the New Organization

The development of the forces of production, industrial structures, transport, and communications since 1945 has emphasized the similarities between the Western nations, particularly between the United States and Europe. Companies, products, customs, and ideas made contact across the Atlantic. Following the law of the alignment of the weaker on the stronger, the Old World tended to align itself on the New: Europe began to be Americanized more swiftly and more deeply than before 1939. But political structures, in part, escaped this general trend. They had always been different, because of the contrast between the presidential and the parliamentary systems, the ideological conflicts of Europe and the lack of ideology in the United States, a more highly developed consensus among the American people, and so on. These traditional differences now began to fade. Presidentialism and parliamentarianism drew closer and closer, until there was no basic distinction between them. Among Europeans, the grip of ideologies diminished and consensus grew—another manifestation of Americanization. But the growth of rigid parties, which profoundly transformed the structure of liberal democracy, involved only Europe; the United States was wholly immune to it. This differentiation in growth between political institutions and the machinery of production was a further illustration of the relative autonomy of the superstructures in relation to the economic foundation.

Rigid Parties

At the end of the nineteenth century, the Socialists had invented a new kind of political organization: the mass party. It entailed educating the working class politically, financing election campaigns and propaganda, and developing democracy in depth. Instead of calling on prominent figures, like the cadre-led parties in the liberal democracies, the mass parties turn to all citizens who are willing to join them. The scheduling of frequent meetings of the members makes it possible to give them political training—the party functions as a sort of night school. The imposition of dues payments on the hundreds of thousands of persons who belong to it gives the party the money for propaganda that the conservatives and the liberals get from the economic oligarchy.

In addition, participation in politics becomes more complete and more direct for all members of the party than in a purely representative system. They determine the directions that it will take, they choose its leaders, they select its candidates for election through the intermediary of the delegates sent by their sections to regional or national party congresses. These democratic mechanisms, however, are partly frustrated by the development of oligarchical tendencies within the parties. The party leaders and candidates are as much co-opted by the incumbent executive committee as they are elected by the representatives of the members, who, in general, approve the recommendations that are made to them. The "full-timers" of a mass party—the militants who are its employees, such as secretaries of branches—naturally wield considerable influence over the organization. This gives rise to an inner circle that exercises the real power under cover of formal democratic procedures. As early as 1912, Roberto Michels minutely described this "iron law of oligarchy" on the basis of an analysis of the Social Democratic party and the labor unions in Germany.

But the effect of this must not be exaggerated. However stable they may be, however powerful, the leaders of the great mass organizations have to reckon with the reactions of the members, who have the last word. No manipulation of a party congress or of its sections can succeed against the solidly asserted will of the rank and file. To possess its confidence is the primary goal of the leaders and their subordinates, and it curbs their autonomy. The party and trade-union oligarchy described by Michels is based, in spite of everything, on elections, which select the members of the oligarchy and can remove them. The economic oligarchy—which he overlooks—is far less democratic. In the Western system, the party and union oligarchy constitutes, in fact, a "counteroligarchy," which strengthens the influence of the citizenry and reduces that of the capitalists.

The party as a whole forms a kind of oligarchy in relation to the public. As a rule, its members are fewer than the voters. But the members dominate the voters because they select the candidates, determine the programs, set up the discipline to be imposed on the men elected, and so on. This occasionally leads to conflict between the inner circle of leaders, chosen by the members, and the parliamentary representatives, elected by the voters. Conservatives often criticize this domination of the people's elected representatives by the party committees and the corresponding transformation of a parliament of individuals into a parliament of organizations. Here again, the situation can be fully grasped only in relation to the power of the economic oligarchy in capitalist systems. Cadre parties offer only feeble resistance to the oligarchy's domination of the representatives, whereas mass parties somewhat loosen its grip. Nor must it be forgotten that every citizen may belong to a party if he wishes. Those who choose not to do so are of their own free will refusing to have a more direct voice in political decisions: they themselves choose to play the part of the passive or semipassive citizen.

The structures thus developed by the Socialist parties were subsequently taken over by the Communists. After 1924, however, the Communists made two organizational innovations. First of all, party members were no longer grouped according to domicile but according to place of employment. The factory cell (or that of the shop, the warehouse, the university) replaced the local section whenever possible. Only the self-employed—such as physicians or lawyers—were still assigned by residence. Second, the Communist parties were organized on the principle of "democratic centralism": decisions were discussed by the rank and file but actually made later at the top and implemented by everyone in a disciplined fashion. The difference was one of degree rather than of kind, since all mass parties tend toward a centralized hierarchic structure.

In certain Western countries, between 1919 and 1939, the Fascists evolved a new type of mass party that combined a classic electoral and parliamentary framework with a militarized organization. Very small base groups (fewer than ten persons), rigidly partitioned and easily moved about, were linked together in a pyramid of many levels. In this way, it was possible to assemble very quickly a few dozen or a few hundred or a few thousand men, as required by the object in view. The members of these groups underwent military training and were armed in varying degrees. The Fascist parties established private militias that were intended to seize power by force and to use violence against their opponents. But they were also electoral organizations that tried to win seats in parliaments, in local assemblies, and in city councils. They

143

never progressed very far except in Italy in the 1920s and in Germany in the 1930s; in these countries they succeeded in overthrowing liberal institutions.

Until 1939, the mass parties played a secondary part in the political life of Western nations, which was based essentially on middle-class parties. The Socialists and the Communists represented "counter-societies," more or less on the border of a system certain of whose fundamental elements they rejected. Between the wars, the Social Democrats took part in some governments; but these instances were exceptional, and the context was that of an intermediate period between liberal democracy and technodemocracy. The latter, in contrast to liberal democracy, was founded essentially on mass parties, or on middle-class parties that had embraced certain features of the mass parties, particularly the rigid discipline imposed on elected representatives.

After 1945, the Christian Democrats and some conservatives attempted to form mass parties. Some of them assembled as many members as the Socialist parties, in a similar system. But the members were seldom militants who took an active part in organizational work; their membership was more formal than real. The inner circle of leaders, made up of prominent figures or professional politicians, played virtually the same part as the committees in the old parties. At the same time, there was another feature of the mass parties: the rigid discipline of its parliamentary representatives. This tended to infect even the conventional parties that were, in other respects, still loyal to their traditional structure. In this, they followed the example of the nineteenth-century British parties, which were the first to practice such discipline. Rigid parties are those that compel their representatives in parliament to vote as a solid group on major questions, whether, in other respects, they be mass parties or middle-class parties.

The spread of rigid parties completely changed the structure of representation and the mechanics of institutions. Voters no longer backed a candidate on the basis of his personal promises, but rather because he was the spokesman and agent of a party. Thus, the real representatives of the citizens were the parties taken collectively, not the members of parliament taken individually. Hence, it was natural that all the legislators belonging to a given party should follow its orders to the letter. Parliamentary debates were of no further value in terms of swaying views, since the votes were decided outside the chamber. Compromises were arranged between party staffs, not between legislators. Ministers were subject to an analogous discipline, so that cabinets acquired the same factitious character. Major political decisions were often taken by the leaders of the parties in coalition, meeting at the highest level. But the government was assured of a majority in parliament as soon as the party or parties supporting it comprised a sufficient number of legislators, since all voted as they were ordered. Consequently, governmental stability was very solid. A new type of Western system, "majoritarian parliamentarianism," came into being.

Most European parties adopted these rigid structures after 1945, whether they were middle-class or mass parties. The French right was the last to fall into line, under the Fifth Republic with the growth of the Gaullist party. Only a few small liberal parties are still holding out against the disciplined party vote. In Japan, the mass parties—the Socialists, the Communists, and the Komeito—are still minorities in contrast to the relatively loose Liberal party, which has ruled the country for a quarter of a century. Hence, the Japanese system is closer to classic parliamentarianism. But the economic oligarchy is very powerful and sustains the Liberals' unity, in spite of their seeming diversity, thus guaranteeing the stability of the government.

Only the United States has clung to the political machinery of liberal democracy. Mass parties have not been able to evolve there, and the traditional middle-class parties have not altered much; they are still as undisciplined as ever. Every member of Congress votes as he sees fit, without yielding to the instructions of his group. The world's most modern nation in the areas of technology and economics thus preserves an archaic party structure, a survival from the nineteenth century, even though the mass parties and voting discipline are in keeping with the development of the forces of production and industrial enterprise, which tend toward big, rigid organizations.

The allergy of the United States to mass organizations and voting discipline is consonant with its visceral preference for decentralization and federalism. Large, rigid parties would, of necessity, be centralizing forces, which Americans do not want. For another thing, the presidential character of their system makes voting discipline and majoritarian parliamentarianism unnecessary, since the government is stable by definition. Rigid parties, in contrast, would hamper the operation of institutions when the president and the congressional majority belong to different organizations. Subordinate factors reinforce the effect of these primary factors: the lack of a large Socialist party, which developed the new structures elsewhere and caused them to spread by infection; the primary-election system, which, theoretically, makes it possible for party members to select candidates; and so forth.

For some years, there has been talk in Europe of the decay of the parties, as, for a century, there has been talk about the decay of parliaments. In actuality, the system of rigid parties continues to rule political life. It is weaker in those countries in which it has always been weaker, such as France and Italy; but even there the parties have become stronger and more disciplined than they were under liberal democracy. Throughout the West, parties remain the basic framework of elections and parliamentary activity, and no one has yet conceived of any substitute that could take over in those basic functions or that could associate the voters more intimately with political life. Attachment to specific parties has declined in proportion to the degree to which the great ideological battles have given way to more technical and more group-based conflicts. Nonetheless, there is no question of a decline of ideologies, though this was thought to be the case in the early 1960s; rather, old ideologies are dying and new ones are still struggling to adapt to the contemporary situation. Indeed, the revolt of the students and other forms of challenge have contributed to a rebirth of ideologies.

The Growth of the Executive and the Weakening of the Legislature

The executive branch is taking the ascendant and the legislative is declining: this dual movement (or, rather, this dual aspect of a single movement) is general. It affects the United States as much as Europe, the tranquil democracies of Britain and the Scandinavian countries as much as the more excitable democracies of France and Italy.

The modifications that characterized this movement affected first of all the legislative power. A number of parliaments have had their freedom of action restricted, notably the French, which under Article 34 of the 1958 constitution has strict limitations imposed upon its powers. The matters on which the French parliament can make laws are precisely stipulated. When constitutions and statutes do not establish similar restrictions, they grow up more or less from circumstances, under various guises. The details of regulation are increasingly left to executive decrees, the legislature limiting itself to the statement of principles. Almost everywhere the assemblies debate only governmental projects: in general, 90 percent of the laws, if not more, are initiated by the executive and not by the members of the parliament. Finally, in several countries the legislature delegates the law-making function to the executive.

The executive's powers to act increased while those of the legislature decreased. In the United States, federal power grew to the detriment of the states, and the presidency gained more than Congress from this. The growth of public administrative entities and agencies stood out in contrast to the stagnation of the House and Senate. A parallel development occurred in Europe. The increase in economic and social services, in nationalized industries, in the apparatus of the state in general has involved spheres and activities that have been brought within the authority of the executive much more than that of the parliament. The complex of administrative and technical instrumentalities at the executive branch's disposal furnishes it with all the data necessary for prediction and decision. Legislatures, on the other hand, are deprived of direct access to such information and can get it only indirectly and with difficulty.

Parliamentary control over the executive has grown correspondingly weaker. In the majority of parliamentary systems, a vote of no confidence is no longer a practical possibility, since the cabinet has a stable, homogeneous majority as a consequence of rigid parties. Seldom— almost never—can the legislature overthrow a cabinet. Ministerial stability is increasing, and the tendency is in the direction of a stable and strong government supported by the legislature. Britain regularly practices this system. Germany, Norway, and Sweden do so almost as faithfully. The average life of a Stockholm government has risen from eighteen months between 1918 and 1939 to thirteen years after 1945: there have been only two premiers in twenty-six years, both members of the same party and leaders of the same majority. Since 1958, France has taken the same road. French deputies who belong to the Gaullist "party" are known to their opponents as "absolutists;" but their colleagues in Britain, Germany, and the Scandinavian countries are equally deserving of this characterization. Legislatures are tending to become depositories for the documentation of decisions made by the general staffs of majority parties.

The shift of parliamentary power to the executive is only one aspect of the change in political organization. The development of the structures of parliament and the executive is also important. Public debate in the legislature, the center of all activity in liberal democracy, has lost much of its importance. It still allows an occasional impressive session in which conflicting lines of argument offer evidence of the Western system's pluralism. Full television broadcasting of some of these sessions gives the citizenry a feeling of contact with them and also forces the members of parliament to exercise some control over their behavior. But the major part of their work nowadays is done in committees or in meetings of parliamentary groups. In Italy, the 1948 constitution authorized this development by endowing the committees with actual legislative power. In the United States, investigating committees and hearings allow some control over governmental activity. European countries are tending to evolve similar procedures.

In a general sense, contemporary parliaments, in order to survive, are increasingly adopting techniques close to those of government. They endeavor to surround themselves with experts and intelligence sources. They set up checks on cabinet officers and the administration through the appointment of independent observers chosen by the members of the legislature. The success of the old Scandinavian institution of the ombudsman is an example. Federal Germany has followed it by establishing a parliamentary military inspector whose task it is to check on the democratic character of the armed forces. Britain has transplanted the institution in a form closer to its original structure. Analogous tendencies are becoming evident in a number of European countries, all in search of methods that will make it possible for the legislature to exert real influence on governments that they can no longer overthrow.

The evolution in the executive branch's structure is, in fact, bringing it closer to these new legislative structures. The president of the United States is surrounded by councils and commissions in which most of the government's decisions are worked out. European governments operate in a similar fashion. Centered on their official meetings, interministry committees, consultative commissions, and working parties multiply; and it is they that prepare the fundamental decisions. The management of a state resembles that of a giant industrial corporation as it has been described by Galbraith. It is in the hands of a collective technostructure that closely links the legislative and executive branches of government behind the mask of their formal separateness. It combines party leaders, ministers, their staffs, committee chairmen, heads of parliamentary groups, influential majority legislators, high career officials, experts, consultants, and so on. This structure is the real ruler of the state.

It is subject, nonetheless, to two outside curbs that restrict its power. First of all, it is more or less dominated by the economic oligarchy in accord with the procedures that have been described earlier; but the oligarchy is naturally most sensitive to those decisions that directly concern it. For example, the political technostructure is freer to authorize student participation in the management of the universities than worker participation in the management of private businesses. Second, it has to consider the voters, whose discipline by the mass media prevents their being completely manageable by the technostructure. The voters' relation to it is somewhat like that of the owners of capital to the economic technostructure. In Europe, where large mass organizations (politicalized unions and parties) embrace many of the citizens, voter pressure is stronger than in the United States.

Despite the convergence of the legislative and the excutive branches and the evolution of a political technostructure, we must not forget that the parliament continues to play a far from negligible part. The necessity of seeking election and reelection affords its members a contact with the electorate that no one else enjoys to the same degree. These elections provide parties and governments with a far better seismograph than opinion surveys. Committee discussions and public debates make it possible to subject drafts to closer scrutiny and to remedy their defects more effectively. They allow for effective restraints on the government through modifications in its proposed budgets and day-to-day criticism of its operations. The legislature, in the end, is the natural forum for the enunciation of discontents and demands.

Oral questions from the floor in the British fashion or other methods of parliamentary interrogation act as safety valves; without them the masses would be far more tempted to violent opposition. Continuing open discussion between parties through their representatives makes it possible to express conflicting points of view. It fortifies pluralism and thus assures the preservation of freedoms. Pressure from members of the legislature compels the executive always to reckon with the national state of mind. Confrontations between legislators and technicians and experts compel the latter always to bear in mind the human factor, which they have a natural tendency to forget. While parliament may never have been the sovereign, basic entity described by theoreticians, while it is no longer the majestic lawgiver of liberal democracy, it is still irreplaceable and important.

The development of Western political institutions evidences a striking parallelism with that of economic structures. Liberal democracy was appropriate to a capitalism of small and medium enterprises founded on individual initiative and competition to win markets. Similarly, politicians vied almost equally freely without any enclosure of themselves or the citizenry within rigid parties. Parliamentary debates could be likened to the stockholders' meetings of industrial and commercial enterprises. This harmony between political institutions and economic structures was broken by the advent of contemporary neocapitalism, based on huge industrial and financial organizations that plan their production in advance and force their products on the consumer through the mass media.

There was a time when it appeared that fascism was representative of this development of the forces of production within a capitalist framework. The transition from a number of parties to a single party in which power is strongly concentrated does correspond to the development of the economic oligarchy in which independent businessmen give way to a centralized structure built on interlocking financial investments. The disappearance of political pluralism closely resembles the accession of large firms to positions of monopoly or oligopoly and the decline of competition. Fascist corporatism, which delegated to the dominant enterprises the task of organizing the various occupations by giving them, in effect, the official power of doing so, was moving in this general direction. Similarly, planning and an economy managed by a state that favored capitalism would destroy the "Reds" and bring the trade unions to heel. And there is a dramatic analogy between the commercial advertising that pushes a product on consumers and the totalitarian propaganda that forces rulers on the citizenry.

And yet, though German Hitlerism—and, to a lesser degree, Italian fascism—was, in effect, analogous to the modernization of capitalism, they reflected only a transitional phase, in which the process of mod-

150

ernization spread confusion among the small factory-owners, artisans, merchants, and peasants, whose existence was threatened by this process. Since 1945, when neocapitalism began to expand, fascism has been on the decline in Western countries. While the danger recurred in France between 1958 and 1962 with decolonization and emerged in the United States in the 1950s with McCarthyism, and while leftist outbreaks revived it in Italy, it was because of the influence of political factors, not economic development. The capitalism of the highly industrialized societies, in the last analysis, seems to accord better with technodemocracy than with fascism.

Collective decisions that bring together in political life experts, technicians, and administrators, on the one hand, and ministers, legislators, and party leaders (and, in economic life, capitalists), on the other, are more in harmony with modern industry than are the individual decisions of a supreme chief. A society based on science and technique is fundamentally opposed to the quasi-military structure of Fascist systems and their mystique of ultrapersonal power. Modern capitalism may resort to fascism when it is afraid of being destroyed by subversion, as it turned to Thiers[1] in 1871, but it cannot adapt itself permanently to it. The rivalries of the oligopolists and the pressures on consumers bear more resemblance to the semipluralism and the semifreedom of the technodemocracies—where a few powerful political organizations compete and the citizen, like the consumer, still has a relative degree of choice—than to the absolute rigid and monolithism of the single party and totalitarian dictatorship.

Types of Political Organization

Technodemocracy's political organization, like its economic structure, becomes increasingly homogeneous. Differences disappear between European parliamentarianism and American presidentialism, between the British and the French parliaments, between northern social democracy and Latin socialism. Nevertheless, these institutions are not yet

1. Adolphe Thiers, French historian and statesman, became interim head of the government after the fall of the Second Empire and the defeat by Prussia in 1871, when the legislature elected him president of the Third Republic.—Translator.

wholly alike. Behind their similarities it is possible to distinguish a number of types of political systems. Side by side with the more or less traditional distinction based on methods of exercising power (presidential, parliamentary, mixed systems), one must point to another, based on the extent of pluralism. The United States, which has only "capitalist" parties, is very different from Britain or Scandinavia or Germany, in each of which there is a large Socialist party, or from France and Italy, each of which has also a large Communist party.

Parliamentary, Presidential, and Mixed Systems

The American presidential system differs from the European parliamentary systems in three major ways. First, the head of the government is elected by the people as a whole and not chosen by the legislature. In form, there is still indirect election, inasmuch as the voters choose electors who, in turn, vote for the president. But in practice, the choice of the electors is made on the basis of only one criterion—the names of the presidential candidates for whom they have promised to vote. The results of the vote by the electoral college have almost always—with two exceptions—been identical with those of the popular vote. In essence the voters directly elect the president. Second, congress, which did not choose the President, cannot force him to resign. The European system of the vote of confidence or the motion of censure does not exist in the United States. Third, relations between the executive and the legislative branches are based on the separation of powers, which guarantees the independence and freedom of action of each. As has been noted, the American executive cannot dissolve the legislature. He cannot raise the question of confidence, that highly effective tool for compelling the legislators to vote for a government bill when the government has a disciplined parliamentary majority. The lack of rigid parties, the individualism of Senators and Representatives, and their tradition of resistance to the presidential power make the Congress of the United States the most powerful parliament in the Western world. Whereas nine-tenths of the laws adopted in Britain originate with the government, a proportion that is virtually universal in Europe, in Washington the number of measures supported by the White House and finally adopted rarely exceeds 50 percent (a figure that was reached in only two years between 1954 and 1968: 1954 and 1965) and at times falls below 40 percent (37 percent in 1957, 31 percent in 1960,

27 percent in 1963). Presidential veto will usually prevent a bill from becoming law. It has been used much more frequently since 1933 than before. Franklin Roosevelt invoked it 691 times, Truman 250 times, Kennedy 25 times, and Johnson 30 times, whereas Lincoln resorted to it only 6 times and Washington twice. But it can be employed only to prevent the adoption of legislation, not to further a reform.

The President has a number of less formal but very effective means of exerting pressure on Congress. In spite of the development of a civil-service system, the spoils system has not been altogether eliminated: Nixon had available some 6500 jobs to distribute after his first election. This made it possible for him to create debts of gratitude toward himself. The awards of government purchases, public-works credits, federal aid, and advantages for this or that large company can be of great importance to certain Senators and Representatives, who can thus be persuaded to back the White House. If the president is popular, his intercession in congressional elections helps candidates whose positions are shaky. Appeals to public opinion by means of press conferences, speeches, and presidential messages can also influence votes in Congress. In spite of everything, however, Congress still possesses far more freedom of action and power of decision than any other parliament in the West.

This is the most important difference between the American and the European political systems. In other respects, modern parliamentary systems tend rather to move much closer to the presidential system. In Britain, West Germany, and the Scandinavian countries, party discipline and the reduction of the number of parties to two (or their alignment in two firm alliances) has changed the significance of legislative elections. These serve not only to choose deputies but also to select the head of the government, who is automatically the leader of the majority party or coalition. The struggle between Wilson and Heath, and between Kiesinger and Brandt, was much like that between Nixon and Humphrey. In each case, the citizens were aware that they were choosing the supreme authority of the state, the real head of the government, and that this choice was the fundamental stake in the electoral battle. Heath, Brandt, and Olav-Palme of Sweden were elected by the citizens, as much as Nixon, Johnson, and Kennedy.

In these same European nations, the executive is no longer overthrown by parliament, in spite of the provisions in the constitutions.

The existence of a disciplined majority and the authority of the chief of government over it eliminate in practice the possibility of a vote of no confidence. The institution is falling into decay. The dissolution of the lower chamber, which was its corollary, is, of course, suffering the same fate. It is employed to set the date for elections at the time that the government thinks is most favorable. It is no longer a means of offsetting the vote of no confidence. It no longer operates to allow the voters to arbitrate a dispute between the legislature and the executive. For there is no conflict now, no vote of no confidence. In practice, the prime minister—British, German, Scandinavian—is assured of lasting as long as the term of the legislature, and this is the equivalent of the American presidential mandate. When the executive's majority is very weak, this stability requires certain special attentions; but it seldom vanishes, even in such circumstances.

Neither the election of the chief of government nor his independence from parliament really differentiates the American chief executive from the European. The basic distinction now derives from the independence of the legislatures with respect to the executive. It exists in the United States, where the executive cannot make Congress yield but can only influence it in some slight degree. It has disappeared in Europe in every country where the parliamentary majority is in the hands of a disciplined, hierarchic party. The leader of the party is also the head of the government. To raise a question of confidence now is to show that the prime minister demands that the deputies of his party vote for him. They are virtually compelled to do so. Any act in breach of discipline would mean the rebel's ouster and would put an end to his political career.

Unquestionably, the leader's authority over his party is never absolute. He has to keep in mind the various tendencies that arise within it, balance them, compromise with them. Discussions and compromises are necessary; but now they take place within the majority party rather than on the floor. Yet, the prime minister has the final word most of the time, if he wishes it, unless, of course, he has committed some very serious political error. In such a case, the party changes leaders and sends the old one into retirement. This was what the British Conservative party did with Lord Avon (Anthony Eden) after the Suez adventure of 1956. When the majority is composed of a coalition, the prime minister's authority is obviously less, unless it is a case of an unequal coalition in which one of the partners is very junior (the Liberals in Germany and the Communists in Sweden with respect to the Social Democrats). In either case, it is necessary to make certain of the loyalty of the junior partner, without whom the government could not remain in power.

Such a situation is midway between the neoparliamentarianism that has been described earlier and a parliamentarianism more consonant with the traditional canons, which is far removed from the presidential system. It has been suggested that the former be called majoritarian parliamentarianism, because it is founded on the existence of a stable, disciplined majority in parliament, such that the same government normally remains in power for the whole term of the legislature and its chief is for all practical purposes put into office by the citizenry through the parliamentary elections. This kind of parliamentarianism is encountered in three kinds of circumstances. The first occurs when there are only two great rigid parties in the country, one of which has the majority of the parliamentary seats, and the small parties are not strong enough to play the arbitrator's part. Such a system is called two-party, and in it the parties' discipline is an essential element of their dualism. In the strict sense of the term, this kind of true two-party system is unknown to the United States where, except for the situation in presidential elections, there are really a hundred parties—two for each state—because of the lack of discipline among the elected representatives.

From the two-party system thus defined, which gives rise to the most solid majoritarian parliamentarianism, one must proceed to two other situations. On the one hand, there is "bipolarization," in which a number of parties join in two stable coalitions, each of which functions in parliament in a disciplined manner. This has been the situation in Denmark, Sweden, and Norway for some years: the three middle-class parties have united against the Social Democrats, each group representing almost half the eligible voters. Reference should also be made to West Germany today, where the Socialists and the Liberals have formed a coalition against the Christian Democrats (the Austrian situation is comparable). In Australia, the alliance of the Liberals and the Agrarians against the Socialists has created a bipolarization of several decades' duration. In each of these countries, governments tend to remain in power for the full term of the legislature, and parliamentary elections make it possible to choose the prime minister from the leaders of the two coalitions. At the same time, internal conflicts can arise and lead to the cabinet's downfall (Norway in 1971), and the coalitions are not always so clearly defined that their leaders emerge clearly at election time (the case of the "middle-class" coalition in Sweden).

A third form of majoritarian parliamentarianism is found in the case of a system of more than two parties in which one enjoys a dominant position; usually it alone claims the majority in parliament, the other seats being held by a number of much smaller groups. India is the best example of such a situation: the Congress party has held the continuing majority since independence, except for a short interval in 1969-70, when Indira Gandhi deliberately brought about a split to slough off the old functionaries who dominated the party machinery. The government is assured of a stable, disciplined majority as long as the legislature sits. It keeps parliament dependent on it. In practice, its leader is chosen by the voters in the legislative elections. There is no true choice then, however, because no real rival can be proposed by the masses. The system acquires a quasi-plebiscitary character. In Sweden, bipolarization is combined with domination by the Social Democratic party: votes were cast in the 1969 and 1971 elections for or against Palme, for there was no clearly designated second candidate. In Japan, the Liberal party is similarly dominant, but its organization is less rigid and less disciplined.

Italy, Belgium, the Netherlands, and France before 1958 were much closer to the traditional parliamentary system. In each country, there were many parties, and they did not establish two rigid, permanent coalitions. Alliances changed from one election to another and, at times, even during the life of a parliament. There were no accepted leaders who automatically became prime ministers in the event of election victories. Hence, the head of the government was chosen not by the voters in the parliamentary elections but by the governing bodies of the political parties. He was never certain of his majority, and he seldom held office throughout the legislature's term. Cabinet crises were more or less frequent but never exceptional. The threat of dissolution regained its original function: it enabled the government to put pressure on the deputies so that they would not force it into the minority. Without becoming ineffective, such a government cannot establish cabinet stability in the absence of a cohesive majority. Once coalitions have been formed, the development of voting discipline makes them less fragile, but their creation is more difficult. While ministries are somewhat less unstable, cabinet crises are usually rather longer, as in the Netherlands or Belgium.

Two variations may be distinguished within this nonmajoritarian parliamentarianism. France between 1947 and 1958 and Italy today resemble the European governments of the between-the-war decades, when it was very difficult to make up a majority, any majority was very brittle and far from cohesive, and governmental instability was high. The average life of a cabinet then was less than a year. (It was six months in the French Third Republic.) The Netherlands and Belgium—as well as Denmark and Norway before the trend toward bipolarization, which is recent and still not too well rooted—are more like the pre-1914 governments, in which alliances were more solid, majorities were less fluctuating, and cabinet crises were less frequent. (The average life of a government is more than a year; in the Netherlands it runs as high as two years.) The distinction is not sharp; it evidences trends rather than well-defined categories.

In this nonmajoritarian parliamentary system, the legislature has considerable power because it selects and removes the chief of government and has him always at its mercy. He has no greater means than does the president of the United States to make the legislators vote for his legislative and budgetary proposals, but he is much more dependent on them for his existence. The French sometimes call this parliamentary type the "assembly system"; in it the legislators' power attains its peak. In certain respects, however, this power is more apparent than real. The power to select the prime minister, to overthrow him, to defeat his proposals, and to vote for others that he opposes does not prevent the legislature from suffering from lack of the technical information available to the minister's staff, from being poorly organized for the study of economic problems, and from working along lines that make it difficult for the assembly to grasp social realities. The Italian parliament today, like the French twenty years ago, is an excellent illustration of the contrast between a seeming omnipotence and a profound impotence.

The French constitutional reform of 1962 pointed to a political system falling midway between European parliamentarianism and American presidentialism, and known as semipresidentialism. In it, the actual running of the government is shared by two persons: a prime minister whom the deputies can force to resign, as in the parliamentary system, and a president elected through universal suffrage, as in the presidential system. Having been chosen directly by the people, the president is not reduced from the start to the purely honorific status of the head of a parliamentary state. He has substantial powers that he can oppose to those of the prime minister; there is a tendency to a two-headed government, a dyarchy. The system is not new, for it was established in 1920 in Germany by the Weimar Republic. Outside France, it is in use today in certain small countries: Austria, Ireland, and Finland. (The Finnish president is elected indirectly, by electors chosen by the voters under proportional representation and empowered to vote for the candidates of their own choice.)

It is difficult to analyze such a system because, as a rule, its experiences have been short and most have taken place in states already put into somewhat peculiar circumstances. In Weimar Germany, only one president was elected by universal suffrage—von Hindenburg, whose training and age did not permit him to carry out his duties in a normal fashion. The storm raised by the economic crisis of the 1930s in any case prevented the normal functioning of institutions. Ireland, too, had only one president elected by universal suffrage, and he was the father of the country, the hero of the fight for independence, old and blind. In Austria, the two big parties that controlled the whole of political and administrative life had virtually made an agreement to put up only colorless, undistinguished presidential candidates who would not annoy the governing groups in the conduct of the state's business. For all practical purposes, the president had no influence, in spite of having been elected by the nation. In France, General de Gaulle transcended the institution, which did not begin to function normally until after the election of Georges Pompidou in 1969.

Only Finland has practiced the semipresidential system for any length of time—half a century. There the special aspects of the election of the head of the state give the party directorates more influence than they would have in a direct vote, and these same circumstances weaken the prestige that would derive from selection by the nation as a whole. The division of power between the president and the prime minister is genuine, and each plays an effective part in the management of the government. When there is a clear parliamentary majority, the president's part is reduced and the prime minister's is enhanced. If the majority is not too cohesive—as is frequent— the reverse is the case. The president's character and personality, too, have some influence on the division of executive power. France's experience since 1969 has not taken the same road as Finland's: although the majority is very strong and very disciplined, the president is the real head of the French government and the prime minister has only a secondary position, though important, in relation to him. This is a consequence of the fact that the majority was first created by de Gaulle and subsequently held together by the election of Pompidou as president.

In the semipresidential system, the parliament's powers seem to depend on the existence or the lack of a strong, cohesive majority within it much more than on the national election of the president. Thus, the subordination of the French National Assembly brings it much closer to the British House of Commons than to the Finnish Parliament, in which there are no stable, disciplined majorities. The distinction, then, between majoritarian and nonmajoritarian parliamentarianism seems greater than that between the parliamentary and the semipresidential systems. The stability of French governments since 1962 owes more to the majority that exists in the National Assembly than to the election of the president by universal suffrage. But the conservation of such a majority seems to depend greatly on such election.

The Range of Pluralism

Pluralism of ideas, of parties, of candidates, of means of expression, and of enterprises is a fundamental element of the Western system. Some observers, indeed, see in it the basic criterion that distinguishes this system from dictatorship, which is characterized by the single party, doctrinal monolithism, and state monopoly of the economy. Like liberal democracy, technodemocracy is pluralist. But it is less so. The propensity for monopoly and oligopoly, for industrial alliances, and for the coordination of firms by means of financial corporations and multiple participations diminishes the pluralism of the economy. The concentration of ownership of the press and of radio and television broadcasting services, and in certain countries the nationalization of all broadcasting, reduces the pluralism of the means of expression. The single local newspaper becomes the rule in the French regional press, and national trusts grow up in Britain, West Germany, and other countries. The information made available by the mass media tends to foster the same ideas, the same themes, the same images, and the same behavior everywhere; this restricts the pluralism of thought and culture.

Political pluralism declines in the same way. At times, this development seems greater than it is. The decrease in the number of parties in West Germany and France gives voters the impression that they have less choice. In actuality, their choice is more genuine, because it has more effect on the formation of governments and because the remaining parties have more chances of action. Similarly, if the development of mass parties makes small groups powerless and the creation of new parties more difficult, this crystallization of views into large popular organizations strengthens opportunities for their expression. The fact remains that the assimilation of the Social Democrats into the Western system has reduced the gap between opposing ideologies. In the majority of European countries, parties thus tend to resemble one another, as in the United States. Opposition is deep only in those nations where there is a powerful Communist party—that is, in Italy, in France, in Finland, in Luxembourg, and in Iceland. Even in these countries, the extent of opposition diminishes and the Communists become less revolutionary.

One must not exaggerate, however. The Communist parties have not yet been assimilated into Western society, as the Maoists claim. They are less inclined to violent revolution and more attached to liberal freedoms: but they continue to reject capitalism completely. Similarly, in spite of the closer relations between Socialist and "middle-class" parties in the Scandinavian countries, West Germany, and Britain, there remains an obvious difference between the two sides. It is less than it was before 1945, unquestionably, but it is still much greater than the difference between the Republican and Democratic parties in the United States. In the area of political pluralism, the fundamental difference does not set off the liberal democracy of yesterday against the technodemocracy of today; rather, it distinguishes between three groups of nations within the two systems: those that have no Socialist parties, those that have Socialist parties but no Communist parties, and those that have both Socialist and Communist parties.

The first category consists exclusively of the United States. Socialism has never been able to rally a large party there that could compete with the two major parties, as it has done everywhere else in the West. The American Socialist party managed to assemble 118,000 members in 1912 and to elect sixty mayors, a number of state legislators, and one member of the House of Representatives, Victor Berger. In 1918, the House refused to allow him to take his seat—a fact that demonstrates the resistance of public opinion to socialism. Weakened by the Communist schism, the party declined thereafter. It almost always put up a presidential candidate from 1892 to 1960, but none of them ever received more than a very low percentage of the vote. In American political life, the Socialist party may be viewed as a minor group expressing marginal opinions that do not succeed in gaining substantial popular support.

Why is the United States so allergic to socialism? The Americans often explain it by their nation's capacity for assimilation, or by the superiority of liberal ideology. But the problem is to learn exactly why America has possessed this capacity for assimilation, why it has believed in the superiority of liberal ideology (which is not apparent, since many Europeans do not accept it). Initially, the influence of earlier consensus is certain. Before the emergence of socialism, Europe had been torn by the antagonism between conservatism and liberalism; ideological division seemed natural. The United States, in contrast, was virtually unanimous; there, ideological differences seemed abnormal. The growth of a new doctrine such as socialism is favored by the first set of circumstances and hindered by the second.

But the driving force of socialism could not have been arrested anywhere if it had the same thrust on both sides of the Atlantic. If equality, liberty, elections, representative assemblies were equally superficial and illusory—"formal" according to Marx—in the United States the pressure of material needs would have led the American workers to take arms against liberalism, as did their brothers in Europe in 1830 and 1848. The weight of history is never heavy enough to maintain consensus when class antagonisms become sharp. The workers of the New World were, like those in Europe, at the mercy of the bosses in a capitalistic jungle. But there were certain elements that made their condition easier to bear and led them to become part of the society rather than move into a radical opposition.

Differences in living conditions do not appear to have been of crucial importance. Few American workers actually attained a middle-class standard of living. The great majority lived under conditions just as miserable as those prevalent in Europe. It has always been terrible to be poor in the United States, and there were many poor people in the period between 1870 and 1939. Yet American society, as compared to that of Europe, *appeared* more open. The European immigrant disembarking in New York had already gone through a kind of revolution by leaving Europe. He was coming to America with the hope of becoming rich. He accepted the notion of profit, that is, of capitalism. There was, to be sure, only a slim chance of his becoming a millionaire. But the rare examples of fabulous individual success became myths that kept hope alive, like the tales of the very rare soldiers of the French Revolution who became marshals of Napoleon's empire.

But it must also be admitted that the immigrant had an excellent chance of raising himself to some extent in the social scale: enough to be able to enjoy some of the middle-class benefits he dreamed of achieving. Furthermore, until at least 1914 American society was kept in balance by a dual movement: economic expansion was continually creating new situations on the intermediate and upper levels of industry, while at the bottom, the unending waves of immigrants contributed a working force to fill the lowest positions. The freshly arrived immigrant took his predecessor's place in the bottom of the proletariat or the subproletariat, while the other moved up to a more acceptable position. But the new arrival knew that there was a term to his own purgatory and that he too would rise, while still another former European would join the cycle. For those who found the rate of climb too slow there was always the possibility of braving the risks of the western frontier. The availability of unoccupied arable land—or land suitable for other uses, such as mining, building, and so on—is an invaluable safety valve for a society. As it snatched such lands from the Indians—whom it exterminated or thrust into reservations—the United States opened a path other than socialism to its proletarians.

From another point of view, those immigrants who had renounced their European pasts felt an overpowering need to be assimilated into the country to which they had come and that they wished at all costs to make their own. Uprooted, bewildered, they were in a psychological state in which American ideas, the American society, the American system constituted their only possible means of attaining stability. To attain an inner equilibrium, a structure for their personalities, they had to enter to the full into their new country, to plunge themselves into the existing community, to accept completely its rules, its morality, its ideology, its values. That the new Americans generally became ultra-Americans merely attested to a general law. Converts are always the most dedicated zealots. Thus, the early generations of immigrants continually reinforced the conformism of the United States, private and public, domestic and political.

In this domain, cause and effect are serial and interactive. The initial conformism of the American people hindered the growth of socialism, the absence of which subsequently strengthened the conformism. Whatever anyone says, ideology is always and everywhere present in the political life of the United States. But it is a matter of a single ideology venerated by everyone, an absolute truth that it would be treasonous to question. Never challenged by an aristocratic counterideology, the liberal ideology was not later defied by a Socialist counterideology. For at least 95 percent of Americans throughout the nation's history, capitalism and elective democracy have constituted dogmas as basic as the existence of God and the power of the United States. Republicans and Democrats were no more than tendencies within a single liberal party, no farther apart than the left and right wings of the British Conservative party or of the German Christian Democrats. Hence, political pluralism was very restricted. Freedom to criticize the government is quite broad as to expression, but very limited as to scope. Apart from a few on the fringes, no one questions the liberal credo.

The range of pluralism is broader in the rest of the West. Undoubtedly, the great battle between the conservatives and the liberals is virtually over in Europe. The German Junkers, the Italian princes, the French aristocrats have lost their political influence. The nobility still enjoys a certain prestige because of the snobbery kept alive by the illustrated weeklies and the sentimental magazines. But everywhere it has come down into the marketplace of business and politics. The peasants, who were so long the class that supported it, have turned away from it as schooling has widened and the influence of the clergy has declined. The great schism of the nineteenth century has ended. Almost everywhere conservatives and liberals have merged in a large "bourgeois" party that is called the Conservative party in Britain, the Liberal party in Australia and New Zealand, the Christian Social party in Belgium, the Christian Democratic party in Germany and Italy, and the Gaullist coalition in France, and that ought in reality to be called the Conservative-Liberal party. A few nineteenth-century liberals have rejected this fusion, but they constitute a very small group. In this respect, Europe has matched the United States, aside from the survival of certain vestiges of the aristocratic ideology in people's minds: money is not the absolute scale of fundamental values, businessmen are less esteemed, their intervention in politics is looked at askance, and so on. But this aspect is definitely secondary.

The fundamental difference between Europe and the United States in the matter of political pluralism arises out of the fact that every European country has a large Socialist party. Although these are being assimilated more and more into the existing order and often renounce the construction of a collectivist economy, they retain a view of the world different from that of liberal ideology. The Social Democrats accept capitalism because of its efficiency. But they dispute its moral value. They remain convinced of the superiority of socialism and they regret that it cannot be put into practice. They are resigned to capitalism, as one is resigned to the mediocrity of life for lack of the power to escape it. Businessmen, managing directors of companies, and owners of the means of production are looked on as necessary evils. Society needs them to assure the growth of the economy. But they are not liked, and they are not ranked at the top of the social scale.

Thus, socialism sustains a basic challenge to the liberal system of values. It always proposes another system in opposition. This is a vital difference from the United States, where only one system of values prevails, except in a few minuscule groups. This coexistence of ideologies changes social relations and mentalities. When European labor unions negotiate with management associations, they are prepared today to enter into more or less long-term collective agreements and to collaborate in the functioning of capitalism; but they continue to regard the employers as aliens belonging to a community other than theirs, embodying opposing values. The assimilation of socialism into technodemocracy is a material assimilation, not a psychological one. Unquestionably, the pressure of the mass media, deculturation, the relative homogeneity of living conditions all tend toward a psychological integration, too. But this is still no more than embryonic. It will require more time for its accomplishment than is generally thought.

Hence, pluralism is more real and more deeply rooted than in the

United States, even in those European nations that are familiar with no other political division than that between middle-class parties and a Social Democratic party. Pluralism is greater still in those countries where there are large Communist parties. These countries are not many, but they are very different from one another: France, Italy, Finland, Luxembourg, and Iceland, to which one ought to add Weimar Germany (1920-1933). The factors that caused communism to develop in some Western countries and to shrink to a marginal group in others are not very clear. It is not possible to draw the line between Latin Europe, which might be considered vulnerable to communism, and northern Europe, which might be thought to be immune to it: Finland, Luxembourg, Iceland, and Weimar Germany are all part of the north. To distinguish between Catholic and Prostestant countries is equally absurd, for the same reason. It is likewise impossible to suggest that the Communist party flourished where the Socialist party was weak and offered less resistance. This would be true of France and Italy but not of Weimar Germany, Luxembourg, and Finland. National factors alone, it would appear, can explain the growth of communism in each individual case.

Be that as it may, the presence of a large Communist party in a Western democracy substantially broadens the range of pluralism. During the 1950s, Stalinism and the cold war had generally led to the isolation of the Communists from the rest of the nation by shutting them into a veritable moral and political ghetto. Thus, one can speak of the great schism of the West. Two radically opposed ideologies confronted each other in a single country: one (communism) wanted to destroy the other (liberalism), which, however, had to accept coexistence in order to perpetuate its own existence. The suppression of the Communist party in a country where it could count on 20 to 30 percent of the votes, where it embraced hundreds of thousands of militants, where it was based on powerful trade-union movements and other mass organizations would, of necessity, have led to dictatorship. Subtle rules were then evolved: in parliaments, Communist votes were counted toward the overthrow of a government but not for its establishment; in the security services (police, army, constabulary) and diplomacy, Communists were barred, but they were kept on in purely administrative branches, universities, and so on. The situation is quite different today. The Western Communist parties are not wholly assimilated into the liberal capitalist system, as their on the left enemies insist. But they reject violence as a means of taking power, and they are willing to play the democratic game of elections and parliaments. They are beginning, too, to recognize the value of political pluralism, which they declare themselves determined to preserve during and even after the transitional phase of building a new society. In the local governments that they control, they have shown themselves to be excellent administrators. In May 1968, they helped confine to Paris an agitation that to them seemed to have no revolutionary prospects. In France and Italy, they seek to participate in leftist governments with the Socialists and a center party (Radicals or Christian Democrats). They did so in Finland in 1966 and 1970.

The Communist parties have not abandoned their goal of destroying the capitalist system and replacing it with a Socialist system. But they have come to recognize that such a change would encounter two obstacles in the West. In the first place, all citizens, including Communist voters and militants, are deeply attached to political freedoms and will accept only liberal socialism. In the second place, the division of Europe decided on by the great powers at Teheran, Yalta, and Potsdam more than a quarter century ago, and respected ever since, precludes the extension of Soviet domination to any Western country and that of Western domination to any Eastern country. A complete seizure of power by the Communists in Paris or Rome would entail immediate reaction by the United States and its allies, as happened in 1945-46 in Greece; an attempt at establishing a liberal, or at least more liberal regime in the East would be strongly resisted by the Russians, as in 1956 in Budapest and in 1968 in Prague. The establishment of socialism in any Western country, then, can be brought about only in a very slow, very gradual, almost imperceptible fashion.

Barring some unpredictable and improbable upheaval in the international situation, it is to be expected that Communist participation in the operations of technodemocracy will evolve in the nations where Communists have a powerful party that contributes to the expansion of pluralism. The presence of Communist ministers in leftist governments in Paris and Rome will one day seem normal. They will be good administrators, with a good sense of the state, as they proved to be after the liberation in 1944-1947. They will be the defenders of their nations' interests against the growing pressure of a multinational economic oligarchy dominated by the United States. Will they in the end be assimilated into a Western system of a new kind, the accession of which they will have furthered, as Social Democracy has been integrated into the existing system that it helped shape? Or will they succeed in preserving their original objectives and slowly constructing a real Socialist system? No one can give a valid answer to this question.

Chapter Nine
Challenge
to the System

At this moment, technodemocracy shows no sign of running out of steam. In spite of the financial difficulties of the United States and the dollar crisis, which has caused repercussions throughout the West, its production continues to rise. Its technical equipment is being improved more quickly than ever, and the proliferation of computers is endowing it with new methods of organization that allow a glimpse into the "postindustrial" society or "technetronic age" whose portrait is painted in such glowing colors by the futurologists. Today (and for the foreseeable future) the per capita scale of living is higher in the West than anywhere else and than ever in history. There is hardly any challenge to political institutions any more, and, while parties are quite rigid, short on dynamism, and lacking in appeal, the zest for political freedom remains, the stronger because of the recognition that in the rest of the world there is less of it.

Nevertheless, the Western system has been in crisis since the end of the 1960s. This is a question not of an economic depression like that of the 1930s but of a spiritual depression. Very active and very small minority groups are challenging technodemocracy as a whole, attacking not so much its methods as its goals. They say that a society wholly oriented to material growth and profit is an inhuman society that precludes any possibility of happiness. They reject the disciplines, the hierarchy, the specialization, the organization implied in the techniques of modern production; and they turn to spontaneity, anarchy, gaiety, poetry. They reject the traditional moral taboos of the West and practice symbolic patricide and sexual freedom at the same time. They search almost desperately for brotherhood and love. They despise wealth, while living in the heart of the world of profit and money.

The silent majority thrusts them off and detests them, but it is strangely responsive to their influence. Secretly it envies them. Apparently they give it a bad conscience. Might the worth and the prospects of the Western system be suspect? Might it be a colossus with feet of clay? Might its staggering economic force, unmatched and still unmatchable, be faced with a moral crisis? At the moment, there is no ground for an affirmative answer. Technodemocracy seems to be very solid, and the challenge that is hurled at it has not seriously shaken it. A few bands of young people and zealots predict its imminent end; writers, intellectuals, journalists descant on its decadence. But the businessmen go on imperturbably with the expansion of their enterprises and their profits. To a great extent, they have "taken over" this defiance, which has provided them with ideas, slogans, and styles for their advertising. Thus, in the end, this rebellion has been made to serve the society that it was intended to destroy.

Rebellion from the Periphery

Technodemocracy is not challenged by major segments of the population, as liberal democracy was by the working class or the old monarchies were by the middle classes. It is attacked from the periphery—that is, by very small groups that enjoy no substantial outside support: the students, the young, the intellectuals, the blacks, foreign workers, and so on. Each of these groups is small, and all of them together constitute, at most, only a strong minority. Only women, whose revolt is the objective of certain liberation movements, approach and sometimes constitute a majority; but they are still only slightly sympathetic to overall challenge of technodemocracy.

Not only are virtually all these groups minorities, but within each the radically rebellious elements are a further minority, which is usually quite weak. A French survey in September 1968, conducted among students just after the May revolt, disclosed that only 12 percent wished to change society radically, while 54 percent wanted reform of the universities and 31 percent wanted to sit for the conventional examinations. Disenchantment in the wake of the defeat of the "student commune" may have reduced the size of the first category; there is every reason to believe that it was never strong. A later French survey, in 1969, presented the reassuring picture of an adjusted, calm generation that indicated how minor were the "class struggle based on age" and the revolt of the new generation. Eighty-nine percent of the young persons questioned said that they were "happy"; of this group, 39 percent claimed to be "very happy" and 61 percent described themselves as "happy enough." (The vagueness of this second qualification, however, leaves the way open to less optimistic interpretations.)

But history is not made by placid, silent majorities. The herd of sheep usually follows the leadership of small minority groups, whether spontaneously or under the impulsion of a sheepdog or a well-managed cudgel. In October 1917, the Russian Communist party had only 25,000 members, and they made the revolution. The proportion of active rebels is no smaller today in many of the Western countries. In the United States, the percentage of blacks who reject all the works of white technodemocracy is certainly much higher. This does not mean that these active minorities will succeed in overthrowing the established order, for many stronger groups have failed at that in the past; but it does indicate that their small numbers are no obstacle in this respect, since equally tiny groups of rebels have occasionally succeeded.

The Student Movements

The climactic point of the student revolts in France was reached in Paris in May 1968. The occupation of the old Sorbonne, of all the university buildings in the capital, and of many of these in the provinces, all covered with black and red flags, in an atmosphere of celebration and revolution, was only the theatrical aspect. What was much more important was the erection of barricades in the center of Paris, which had not happened since the 1871 commune, except during the liberation fighting of 1944, in which the antagonists were Frenchmen and foreign soldiers, not Frenchmen alone. The importance of this was emphasized by the fact that the most solid government that France had had for a quarter century, after ten years in power under the leadership of a national hero, had been rocked to its foundations. Some observers believe that a true revolution had been launched and might have overthrown the capitalist system. This seems dubious. However, General de Gaulle's fall more than a year later was certainly the result of an event from which French society has not yet recovered.

Student movements had even more serious political consequences in nineteenth-century Europe, where they were often the incitements to liberal revolutions. Today, they sometimes have equally important results in Third World countries. But at the end of the 1950s, no one would have supposed that they could play the same part in the highly industrialized nations, which were apparently stabilized, integrated, and, therefore, rendered immune to revolutionary processes. Yet, the newest student agitation began in the most highly developed country, where social integration seemed the greatest and the danger of revolution the slightest: the United States. It began in 1960 in the black colleges in the south, where the students initiated the drive for racial integration by nonviolent means. Other universities joined the movement out of sympathy: the Student Nonviolent Coordinating Committee was established in April 1960 and Students for a Democratic Society came into being in June. The struggle for racial equality meshed from the start with the campaign against American imperialism: the war in Vietnam, the policy toward Cuba, intervention in the Dominican Republic, and so on. This campaign was substantially enlarged by the extension of the draft for manpower for the fighting in Indochina.

In the same year, 1960, trouble erupted in the universities of Japan. Ignited by the Japanese-American security alliance, it was directed essentially against the imperialism of the United States. The agitation was led by a very strong, highly structured, tightly disciplined student organization, the Zengakuren. It took the form of urban guerrilla warfare waged by helmeted militants equipped with shields, clubs, and Molotov cocktails. The occupation of university buildings was a secondary affair, though sometimes they were transformed into veritable strongholds that the police had to take by storm after violent combat. There was a great difference between this and the nonviolent character of the early American university actions. But nonviolence began to decline in America in the face of brutal police repression and the radicalization of the blacks' struggle for racial equality. The methods of the Zengakuren were emulated in every Western country, but students there did not succeed in bringing into being any organization so powerful.

Rebellion in the universities began later in Europe than in the United States and Japan. It started in 1966 in the Free University of West Berlin, and the trigger was the struggle against the war in Vietnam. Leadership came from the Sozialistische Deutsche Studentenbund (SDS—the same acronym as the American student organization's, but not the same meaning: the German group is the Federation of Socialist

German Students), an old organization of student Social Democrats that had been expelled from the party in 1960. Its chief was a remarkable man, an excellent speaker and manipulator of crowds, Rudi Dutschke. In demonstrations against the war in Vietnam and subjection to the United States (at the time of Vice-President Humphrey's Berlin visit in 1967) and advocating the democratization of the university, the SDS led the assault on the Springer press trust, which was gradually establishing a monopoly over the large-circulation newspapers of West Germany, forcing them to enunciate an ultraconservative policy and calling for lynch-mob justice for the student revolutionaries, just as the Nazis had done with the Jews. The battle was intense. A leaflet distributed by "Commune No. 1" seemed to be a call for the burning of the great department stores. In 1967, a student was shot to death at point-blank range by a policeman, who was acquitted. Dutschke was the victim of an attempted assassination by a right-wing extremist on April 11, 1968. In retaliation, a number of student riots broke out in German cities—Munich, Frankfurt, Hanover, Cologne, Stuttgart, Essen, as well as West Berlin—and there were two deaths. Dutschke's retirement (he still is in poor health and has to abstain from all political activity) and the movement's excesses led subsequently to a backlash.

In the same year of 1966, university agitation spread to Italy, where it reached its height in 1967-68 with the occupation of university buildings and street demonstrations. The Italian trade unions were less hostile than the German and American labor organizations to the student movements, but still they had strong reservations. Britain and the Scandinavian countries were the only parts of Europe not affected by student revolts. The London School of Economics did experience a strike, and buildings were occupied, but Oxford and Cambridge were islands of tranquillity. There was a surge of fever at the University of Stockholm in May 1968, but it was very limited. The agitation at Louvain in Belgium had a certain nationalist character, like that in Montreal a few years later.

The French student revolution of May 1968 may be regarded as the sequel and the peak of earlier agitations. Until then, no university rebellion had crossed the boundaries of a city, or gone beyond sporadic demonstrations in a few cities. What occurred in Paris assumed a national character with the general strike that it set off. But the movement did not control the strike. The labor unions and the Communist party retained their grip on the working class, whose demands were reformist and not revolutionary. The student revolt having thrust the government into a position of weakness, the workers exploited the situation to gain improvements in their living conditions. "Worker-student" solidarity was a myth, except in a few enterprises where there were a large number of young or foreign workers. The situation was not revolutionary, as the student leaders thought or pretended to think it was. The whole thing ended with the victory of the right in the elections of June 1968.

After the great gala of May in Paris, agitation in the West declined. But it did not vanish; it remained latent everywhere. Some students took part in purely university reform or supported less revolutionary political groups: Liberals, Socialists, Communists. Some took refuge, on the other hand, in the small, more violent group that systematically had recourse to provocations and even assassination attempts. Still others sought close links with the workers, themselves becoming workers, as the worker-priests had done just after the war. Apart from sporadic crises, the universities in general are now calmer. But the students no longer feel that they are an integral part of the society. It would probably require very little to set off new explosions.

All the Western student movements have certain characteristics in common. They are deeply concerned with domestic social problems. Purely university problems, most important in Italy and France (where higher education seemed more anachronistic), were never of the first importance. They are always posed as the consequences of the social situation as a whole. The authority of professors, the examination system, attendance control, and disciplinary regulations are the university's expression of the repressive nature of the society. The oppression and the alienation that afflict students are specific instances of general oppression and alienation. The transformation of the university is impossible without the transformation of the society. Thus, the university movements end up criticizing capitalism and advocating socialism. In the United States, they have been slower in taking this road; but they have entered on it, nonetheless.

Student socialism is closer to utopian socialism of the 1848 variety than to Marxism, though it is often invoked. Most of the rebellious students reject the hierarchic organization of the Social Democratic and Communist parties in favor of small autonomous groups in which spontaneity prevails. Their dream is of an economy founded on the same structure: units managed by the workers themselves, each unit independently planning its own production and making contracts with the others. Even Maoism, adapted to agricultural or semideveloped countries, is a utopia in comparison with Western societies. The "worker-student" alliance is sought after with passion but seldom found. Everywhere the labor unions are distrustful, indeed, frankly hostile; they are less so in Italy than in the United States or Germany, but the difference is not too great.

Student movements also give a great deal of attention to international and imperialist problems. The war in Vietnam, the situation in Cuba or the Dominican Republic, and the exploitation of the Third World often act as triggers and always play important parts. This emphasis is greater when the students are directly concerned (for example, with the draft in the United States), for then the leaders find much more receptivity in the mass of students. But outside problems are very important, even when there is no such direct interest. Students seem to have become aware of a fundamental datum of the modern world: the international class struggle, which opposes the industrial and the proletarian nations.

Sexual problems, finally, are seldom absent from student movements, to the delight of the psychoanalysts and the shock of the general public. To a certain extent, they represent a conscious, planned provocation; it is to be noted that in the United States the student revolt went through a phase of acute obscenity that was also present in varying degree elsewhere. But the call for sexual freedom goes far beyond this provocative character. It is real and deep. It expresses a direct alienation, more profoundly felt by the young, who have little experience of privations. It is part of the dream of a fuller, richer, more developed life, in opposition to a "one-dimensional" society based on money and profit. The anarchist aspect of the student revolt, its rejection of all rules, its "spontaneism," its flexibility are all part of the same attitude, which is to be seen also in the revolt of other minorities.

The Other Rebelling Minorities

Some observers speak of a generational class struggle, the students representing the most aware and active segment of their generation. But the young are not a social class, and the rebels among them constitute only very weak small units outside the universities, where, for that matter, they are not very powerful. In Europe, however, young workers are more receptive than their elders to radical movements. They are often behind "wildcat" strikes—that is, strikes called in defiance of union discipline. Their material situation is harsher in terms of housing, wages, and jobs. Very often, like the blacks in the United States, they are the first to be dismissed in an economic recession. In a more general way, participation in the life around them confronts them with difficult problems that adults do not experience. In France, the advances in farming have compelled the young peasants to break away from the traditional circumstances in which they spent their childhood; the cruel transition from the rustic world to city living uproots their existence.

The hippie movement represents a deeper and more comprehensive revolt. It involves only a small number of young persons, but they have the broad sympathy of the others. By way of their long hair, their imaginative clothing, their pop music, their shared sensitivities and attitude to life, the young in the West have developed a common set of values. Their point of departure is a radical rejection of a society based on money and profit; in other words, of the Western system. Poverty and the equal sharing of everything in their fraternal communities are reminiscent of certain aspects of early Christianity. They, too, are reacting against a society that is quite similar to the late Roman Empire, except that the barbarians are no longer—or not yet—capable of breaching the "frontier." Drugs, Hindu myths, the mirage of Katmandu also represent a flight into dream to escape an unbearable reality. Not all the young use drugs or play at Buddhism, but many feel a secret or admitted sympathy with their brothers brave enough to flee a stifling world.

However marginal the hippies may be, they have already exercised considerable influence on art and culture. In music, the theater, cinema, and literature, they have brought about the emergence of a "counterculture," breaking with traditional forms and content. In part, this has to do with an exploitation of their activities by an industrial society that transforms them into consumer goods: records, films, books, clothes, toys, and so on. But at the same time, this makes possible an impressive diffusion of the counterculture, which penetrates everywhere and recruits new disciples. Who, in the last analysis, is taking over whom? For the moment, most of the young seem still to be quite properly behaved, willing to be assimilated into technodemocracy after certain sacrifices to the rites of passage. But there is no evidence that things will not take a different course one day.

The "clerks" constitute another minority in revolt. This term means first of all the intellectuals, the scholars, the writers, and the artists, everyone whose job it is to think and to express. In Europe, they have often played a quite important part in society since the cultural revolution of the eighteenth century. As a rule, they have challenged the existing order. Initially, they favored liberalism against the monarchist systems, then socialism against the capitalist system. Their system of values has always been opposed to privileges of birth, to wealth, and to profit and friendly to the equality of man, to free development, to indifference to material possessions, to the quest for quality in life—in other words, very close to current themes. Some observers have remarked that the hippie and student movements have brought surrealism back to life after fifty years.

Until recently, intellectuals in the United States were more conformist and less influential. Yet, the opposition to atomic armament that arose among American scientists after 1945 had its roots in a liberal Protestant tradition. But such political action by the "clerks," in the European fashion, also showed some new characteristics. The liberary movement of the "beatniks" in the 1950s, led by Allen Ginsberg and Jack Kerouac, expressed a deeper and more thorough break with American society that preceded the defiance by the young and probably contributed to its coming into being. The explosion of artistic experiment of which New York is the center, unseating Paris as the capital of innovation, parallels the ascension of the United States as a dominant power and is, at the same time, a radical challenge to its way of life.

"Clerks" must be taken to mean also the real clerks in the initial sense of the word—the churchmen. Most of them have remained loyal to the established order, following tradition. In general, the bishops and the upper clergy are conservative. Among priests and pastors, a minority—composed especially of younger men—has aligned itself with the rebels. In the rejection of money and profit and self-interest, in indifference to wealth, in the search for real community, these clerics see the rebirth of basic Christian values. Even sexual liberation does not seem wholly culpable to them in the degree in which it breaks with hypocrisy and seeks love. Against the background of the general decline of all religion in the West, one may thus observe among the young a rebirth of centers of intense Christianity, far removed from recent traditions but close to the early churches, even in their rebellious character.

Other minorities in revolt, or capable of revolt, are more special categories, the oppression of which is more specific because it is more material. This is the case of the American blacks. They constitute the greatest potential revolutionary force in the Western world. For them, racial inequality is compounded by social exploitation. This subproletariat functions as a reserve of cheap unskilled labor and a ballast of unemployed workers. The burgeoning of its class-consciousness is stimulated by its determination to rise above the humiliations of several centuries and to insist on its own African culture. Thus, even more than the nineteenth-century European proletarians, the blacks tend to constitute an alien nation within another nation and arrayed against it. Their position as a majority tends to make the inauguration of a white fascism more probable than any other solution in the event of a dramatic confrontation. In this respect, technodemocracy is more fragile in the United States than in the other Western nations.

In other countries, the equivalent of the American blacks is the foreign workers. But they are less numerous and, above all, not so deeply rooted. They remain foreigners; that is, they do not have the right to vote or often that of labor-union protection, and they are constantly at the mercy of expulsion on the order of the police. Yet, however lamentable their material situation may at times be, it is generally better than it would be in their home countries, where their families live on the money that they send back. Exploited occasionally as native workers were in the nineteenth century, they have virtually no means of resistance and consequently little revolutionary potential. Moreover, local workers tend to be jealous of their competition, as white workers are of blacks' competition in the United States. Thus, a certain racism flourishes in the European lower classes.

It is difficult to mobilize this subproletariat for political action, as some young leftists try to do. By laying bare this new form of imperialism, which acquires larger and larger dimensions in industrial societies, they contribute willy-nilly to the creation of a bad conscience among their compatriots. If massive resort to imported labor forces continues and increases in the highly industrialized countries, as appears likely, there is the possibility that the foreign workers will gradually achieve a certain unity and strength that will enable them to exert pressure on the system.

Other minorities are harshly oppressed: the crippled, the ill, the old, and, in a general sense, the lower fringe of the population, which makes up the 15 to 20 percent of the "poor" who are left out of the consumer society—they are not all blacks or foreigners. It may be expected that their number will decrease as the economy progresses. But there will always remain an irreducible minimum of the unemployable, the unlucky, or, more simply, people who are more vulnerable, less intelligent, less socially adaptable than their fellows. A social-service apparatus and planned retirement can perhaps make their lives more bearable, as has happened in certain countries such as Sweden. In Europe, the Socialist and Communist parties are working hard to improve their lot. In the United States, the lack of such parties and the liberal tradition threaten to delay the solution of the problem still longer. In any case, it is no menace to the Western system, because these marginal citizens are too weak and too lacking in energy to challenge it.

A far more important category of the oppressed, since it embraces half the population and occasionally more, could exert great political power: women. Though their position in the West is better than in the East, it is still full of inequalities. Even the American matriarchate conceals a state of inferiority. In the United States, as in Europe, women are generally paid less than men for the same work. With few exceptions, they are employed in auxiliary or subordinate positions, if not indeed only in fields that are presumed to be "women's work." In a survey of women's political influence made twenty years ago for the United Nations' Economic, Scientific, and Cultural Organization, it was found that the barrier here, as in every other area, was essentially cultural. It derives from the fact that the man is regarded as polyvalent—that is, capable of doing anything—and the woman as monovalent, or specialized in a small number of precisely demarcated fields, and that she herself accepts this stereotype imposed by a system of values set up by men.

The "postindustrial" society finds more profit in turning women into consumers than in enlisting them in production. The number of women with working skills tends to decline in the West, where advertising is completely centered on woman as a figure reduced to the level of a buying-machine and seeks to make her as insatiable as possible. By so doing, it thrusts her further into the infantile, dependent psychology from which her vocational responsibilities tended to rescue her. At the same time, the advertising aimed at men seeks to make the woman an erotic object, a flirtatious doll, titillating and submissive. The women's publications persuade their millions of readers that in this inferior position they will lead the best possible lives if, as the result of a few psychoanalytic consultations, they learn a sexually enticing behavior that will help them to deserve from their husbands a greater regularity and ingenuity in the performance of marital duties.

So thorough an indoctrination makes it difficult for the mass of women to be responsive to the challenge posed by the feminine liberation movements that are growing in the West. These movements represent a very small minority, even smaller in proportion than the student and youth movements. Their dramatic aspects occasionally overshadow the fact that this is a struggle against genuine and far-reaching oppression. The emphasis placed on sexual freedom owes its origin only in part to provocation: women's inequality in this field is greater than in others. A woman's adultery is more harshly viewed than a man's. A man of sixty with a girl of twenty evokes smiles: a woman of sixty with a boy of twenty evokes gasps. In 1969, in France, a woman of thirty-five was thrown into prison and driven to suicide because she wanted to live with an eighteen-year-old boy. Catholics' reactions to papal denunciations of contraception show, moreover, that women are aware of these problems. However, they seem less inclined to rebel against society as a whole than against a single segment of society.

Revolution or Regulation?

Before the rebellions of the 1960s, it was thought that revolution had become impossible in the West. The rise in the scale of living seemed to be wiping out social tensions and making class conflict less violent. The workers were apparently afraid that sudden upheavals might drag down their living conditions. The belief in democracy, pluralism, and political freedoms afforded an impetus toward negotiation and compromise rather than open confrontation. A radical change in structures was still possible in spite of this growth of consensus, but only, it was believed,

179

through a long process of cumulative reforms, each carried out in a peaceful, legal fashion. Even a revolutionary objective, it was thought, could henceforth be achieved only through reformist means.

This theory has since been thoroughly invalidated. The rebelling students of Berkeley, Berlin, and the Sorbonne; the hippies and the young New Left; the women's liberation organizations; and the progressive intellectuals regard the movement born in 1960 in the Western universities as the first phase of a revolutionary process that is going to destroy the Western system. Many compare the Student Commune of 1968 with the Workers' Commune of 1871, the inspiration and model for the October Revolution of 1917. The fact that the two latter events were separated by forty-six years may somewhat reassure the capitalists of Europe and the United States, although the acceleration of history may hasten the maturation of situations. It remains to be seen whether the revolt of the periphery can really culminate in a revolution, or whether it will prove to be merely an illusion.

The Illusion of Revolution

The theory of revolution by the outsiders was evolved by a German-American philosopher, Herbert Marcuse, who influenced the student revolts in Berkeley and Berlin and, almost after the fact, that of May 1968 (his works had only just been translated into French and their circulation was still extremely limited). It is based on the idea that capitalist industrial society, founded on economic growth, the quest for profit, and the conditioning of consumers, gives rise to a feeling of frustration. Once the superficial satisfaction that comes from comfort and gadgets has passed, man feels mutilated in this "one-dimensional" universe, in which he is reduced to the position of a consumer of things for which he feels no real need. He dreams of a more varied, more profound, more humane world in which he could develop his potentials to the full. What now interests him more than material abundance is the elimination of the prohibitions that paralyze him and the destruction of a society that represses basic human instincts. Instead of suffocating organizations and structures, he is looking for a life that is total by reason of its spontaneity, its fantasy, its poetry, its eroticism.

Marcuse believes that the mass of Western citizens is not yet aware of this situation. The students, the young, the women, and the intellectuals feel it more keenly. They are few in number in relation to the whole of the population, without which they can accomplish nothing. But their activity helps to acquaint it with its own alienation. At the start their revolt performed a revelatory function. It found allies in other peripheral groups, thrust outside the consumer society, whose alienation assumed more traditional forms: the blacks, the imported workers, the poor, the unwanted. Together they represent a formidable detonator that can set off chain reactions capable of blowing the Western system to bits. On these ruins, a truly human society could be built and freely and spontaneously developed without any preconceived plan.

Marcuse's theory did not grasp the weakness of the "outsiders." The students, the hippies, the New Left groups, the intellectuals, the women's liberation forces, the foreign workers, and the rest do not amount to much numerically in relation to the size of the population. Above all, they are very diversified groups that have hardly any common interests and goals. It seems quite unlikely that they can overthrow a powerful, rich, organized society, most of whose members are opposed to them. The revolt of May 1968 seemed to come close to overthrowing a solidly established government. But this was an illusion. The forces of order never really went into action. (The police never fired a shot.) If they had acted, the students would have been incapable of resisting. The workers' general strike had reformist objectives (better wages and working conditions, and so on) and the unions refused to join a revolutionary attempt that to them seemed doomed.

The extent of the rebellion was exaggerated by the press, the radio, television, and the other mass information media. To seduce readers, listeners, and watchers every day, one must endow the moment with a form and colors that it seldom possesses. The most picturesque elements profited more than the others from this approach: the student revolts, the hippie communities, the intellectuals' manifestos, the women's liberation extravagances, the sexual provocations, and so forth. At times, events themselves were distorted by the instruments of the mass media. On the barricades in May of 1968, the students followed with their transistor radios the live coverage of their operations that was being broadcast by various stations, and they modified their actions accordingly. Even Achilles, had he heard Homer describing his exploits as the battle raged, would have altered his tactics and perhaps his strategy. The extent of the rebellion was therefore dependent on the

181

notion of it given to the public rather than on its own reality. In sociology, things are not merely what they are; they become to some extent what they are believed to be.

Marcuse, furthermore, did not think the revolution was quite so near as his partisans believed. For the detonator of peripheral revolts to blow up society, it is necessary that a large part of the population be aware of its alienation. The world is still far from that. To be satiated by the consumer society, one must first be a part of it. This is not the case for the majority of Europeans and for a large part of the American population. The rebellion of the young and the students is especially strong in the respectable middle class, because this group is not beset by the material problems that others still contend with. What is more, even when it has become aware of the mutilations that the "one-dimensional" society imposes on it, the West will not abandon that society unless it has a reasonable assurance that a multidimensional society can be established quickly.

To tell people that it will spring out of their own uncurbed spontaneity is not enough. They are not persuaded by an assertion so contrary to experience. No human growth is possible in a world of scarcity, and scarcity has been overcome only by the tremendous technical organization of highly industrialized societies. Let this organization collapse or be seriously weakened, and poverty will be reborn. The hippie communities are by-products of economic development. They could not survive if they were not surrounded and sustained by its productive apparatus. Without it, their relative poverty would be no longer voluntary but enforced. Above all, this poverty would become permanent and absolute, without the safety nets that it has today.

The basic weakness of the rebel movements derives not so much from the small number of their participants as from the fact that they have no direct relation with the growth of the forces of production. To say that the French revolt of May 1968 was a psychodrama or a game is to miss the fact that its participants were not playing and that, on the contrary, they felt that they were living more wholly and deeply than ever before. Objectively, however, what they did resembled theater or a game because it was outside the realm of production. They themselves were aware of this in a certain way. Their determination to unite the students with the workers was the expression of a pathetic anxiety in this respect. The notions of the "new working class" seem to tend in this direction. In a radical form, it asserts that technicians, scientists, and intellectuals have become the essential force in modern production and, therefore, the driving force in social conflict. It proclaims that "the working class continues to increase, incorporating into itself increasingly large sectors of intellectual workers."

In any case, these theories deal only with the students and not with the other peripheral groups. But the students are not yet part of the "new working class," however valid the definition of it may be. They will belong to it only in the future. Meanwhile, their activity is not directly productive. An interruption of the universities and the laboratories could affect production only several years later, by depriving it of the technicians and researchers of the future. Revolutions are not made by such slow processes. The Western system does not appear to be seriously endangered by them.

The rebels' isolation from the forces of production is likewise evidenced on another level. The cultural revolution of the eighteenth-century philosophers was not a game because its ideas and its plans corresponded to the economic and technical development of the society in which it was taking place. The Chinese cultural revolution of 1966 was not a game because it too was in harmony with the conditions of production in contemporary China. The cultural revolution of the California hippies or the Parisian students of May 1968 was a game because it turned its back on the forces of production in the modern West and on their probable evolution. To revive the Christian communities of the early centuries or imitate the Indian ashrams, to dream of mini-socialism on the 1848 model based on the free association of small units of collective production—all this is absolutely alien to the contemporary industrial economy, even if sexual freedom were to be accepted.

If one day, the majority of the West's population should become aware of the alienation in which it is imprisoned by the "one-dimensional" society—an alienation that is genuine and profound—it is doubtful that it will emulate the revolutionary pattern of the peripheral groups, at least while they remain outside the productive apparatus that supports mankind's material existence. This does not mean that Western society has no reason to fear—or to hope for—a revolution; but it does mean that, if a revolution does come, it will be of another kind. The quality of life and its multidimensional character can be developed only if there is assurance of the physical supplies essential to life and its material foundations. The problem is not that of *replacing* today's technical society with a civilization of spontaneity, growth, eroticism, and poetry, but rather of *adding* the second to the first: otherwise a relapse into misery, suffering, and violence is inevitable. The current rebellion does not address this problem, and thus it cannot be truly revolutionary, even if it contributes to the maturation of a revolution that will be carried out by others.

Regulation and Assimilation

The revolt from the periphery, on the contrary, takes on some conservative and indeed reactionary aspects. The students' hostility to strict control of curriculum and to any kind of selection is a rejection of the technical evolution of industrial societies, which insists on the systematic search for the most gifted and competent persons and endows them with mounting social authority. The students' attitude corresponds rather to primitive capitalism, under which anyone at all can found and develop an enterprise if he has a little ingenuity and a little initiative. If universities were organized on such bases, the devaluation of their diplomas would deprive the most intelligent and the best-endowed graduates of their opportunities. Ascent in the social scale would depend on family connections and therefore would be conservative. The American blacks who learn some African language or become converts to Islam to rediscover their identity are also thrusting their racial brothers in the direction of regression rather than of progress. They are locking them more firmly into their ghettos and their underdevelopment.

Rebellion can become reactionary in a still more dangerous manner. While the economic structure of technodemocracy is very solid, its political structure is less so. Any liberal system is fragile if it is founded on tacit agreement among the citizens to a set of rules necessary to social life. Without self-discipline and respect for others, democratic institutions can no longer function, and capitalism turns to dictatorship in order to survive. In the mass of the population, the violence and provocation of certain far-left groups arouse a growing apprehension of disorder and anarchy. If this new fear of the "Reds" were to develop, technodemocracy would be in danger of giving way to a techno-autocracy for which, in the 1930s, fascism afforded the first model. In this respect, the United States appears to be in greater peril than the other Western countries because of the black minority's power. Elsewhere the danger seems still to be minor, in direct proportion to rebellion itself. The growth of neofascism in Italy, however, is evidence that it must not be underestimated.

In a broad sense, the revolt from the periphery strengthens more than it weakens the society. Instead of pushing the Western societies towards the left, as the leaders of these groups desire, they might on the contrary push them to the right. But it is even more likely that the rebellion of the marginal groups would lead to a stabilization and strengthening of the established order. It would do this in two ways: one may be called assimilation and the other regulation. The first involves the ability of technodemocracy, like all other expanding systems, to turn to its advantage the means used by its adversaries in order to destroy it. In political terms, for instance, technodemocracy uses the agitation of the leftists to scare the silent majority and make them vote according to its wishes. The Student Commune of Paris was responsible for giving to the French National Assembly a Gaullist majority in 1968. Since then, it has become customary to plant in these small revolutionary groups policemen and provacateurs who exploit them by reviving agitation on the eve of an election or when the government is in difficulty, thus frightening the silent majority into providing the desired result at the polls.

At the economic level the ability to assimilate the opposition is even greater. Liberal democracy managed to bring Christianity into line with the Puritans' ethic of enrichment and propensity to invest; it identified the secular with the spiritual, as symbolized by the Bank of the Holy Ghost. Technodemocracy is even more versatile. It utilizes revolutionary art, sexual liberty, the protest of the intellectuals, and student movements to develop consumption and to increase the profits of the economic oligarchy. Youth becomes a large market for records, films, transistors, books, clothing, gadgets, magazines, cigarettes, drugs, and so on. Rebellion sells well, from the posters of Che Guevara to pop music and hippie fashions. It sells well even among the older persons who want to follow the action. Advertising uses the themes, forms and symbols taken from the "rebels"—for instance, the exploitation of the erotic and the psychedelic.

The rebellion of the marginal groups also tends to correct some of the basic defects of the Western system and make it more acceptable, or at least less unbearable; it thus serves as a sort of regulator. This phenomenon of regulation can be observed on at least three levels. First, the rebellious movements lessen the sclerosis and rigidities that naturally develop in the large hierarchical organizations so characteristic of technodemocracy: mass parties, large trade unions, giant enterprises, huge administrative machineries. The members of these organizations come under the control of a small group of leaders who are recruited on the basis of co-optation and who hold to the established methods and resist change. In private firms, competition and the search for profit produce an innovative force which acts as a counterweight. But in the parties, in the trade unions, in political administration this counterforce does not exist and the leadership groups become more closed and less responsive. The small marginal groups of rebels are too small to compete effectively with these large organizations. But they can act from within by developing a pressure that forces the leaders to take into consideration the rank and file. In Europe the growth of working-class groups, farmers' associations, the Social Democratic parties, and even the French and Italian Communist parties has been influenced by the action of the marginal groups. Their rebellion might largely correct one of the most serious defects of technodemocracy by providing a permanent counterforce to the established apparatus. The constant stream of younger people recruited by these organizations provides also the best means of preserving them from sclerosis and rigidity, that sociological form of the deterioration of human energy.

The rebel groups assure regulation of the Western system in another way: they provide a safety valve. It has been said that their manifestations resemble the Roman Saturnalia or the Feast of Fools that in earlier times contributed to the maintenance of social equilibrium. That the slaves were allowed a few days equality with their masters and the freedom to act as they please, that simple monks took the place of bishops to conduct religious services and render justice, that the people escaped from the usual constraints and rules for a short time—all these made it easier to cope with inequality, masters, lords, and rules the rest of the time. The hippie communities, festivals of pop music, Latin Quarter Saturday nights, occupations of universities, street-fighting, the Parisian barricades of 1968, guerrilla theater, and sexual freedoms render the same service today to the Western societies. They introduce fantasy and feast, play and color into a world which has been deprived of them. They bring a spontaneity, a community, a warmth, a feeling of well-being—in short, a feeling of humanity—to a frozen, rigid, antiseptic, and computerized society. Thus rebellion feeds into the hubs of Western societies the oil that makes their wheels turn more easily. And it does so not only at rare intervals. It begets a counterculture and a countermorality that transform, rejuvenate, and revive Western culture. The upheaval in customs, habits, and ways of expression that began in the 1950s, notably with the Beatles, was revolutionary in terms of day-to-day life, but not in the social and political sphere, in which, rather, it reinforced the established order by endowing it with new warmth, spontaneity, and opulence.

Finally, rebellious groups carry to their conclusions those liberal principles that are at the foundation of the Western system. Sexual freedom, for instance, even if contrary to the traditional taboos, is a direct extension of liberalism. It is a freedom like all others. It appears more shocking than freedom of thought because it is new. But freedom of thought was equally shocking in the eighteenth century. By emphasizing love without marriage, human brotherhood, contempt for wealth, and generosity the "rebels" in fact restore the essence of Christian morality.

Moreover, the rebel counterculture and countermorality provides, all unwittingly, an ideology that the technodemocracies now need. The primacy of the search for maximum income is natural in a capitalist society where the quantity of goods produced does not meet the demand and where the rich themselves retain a feeling of uncertainty about their wealth in the midst of the poverty that threatens them. But the more society approaches a stage of relative abundance for all citizens, the more they begin to feel liberated from the burden of work and production. Having satisfied their material needs, they begin to give precedence to the pursuit of a better quality of life, to precisely those experiences extolled by the counterculture and countermorality. Thus, the rebellious groups provide an ideology that capitalism needs to divert attention from the inhumanity of the capitalist system.

Yet despite assimilation and regulation, in the last analysis the rebellious groups undermine the Western system more than they reinforce it. Some of them radically challenge the basis of economic success of the system, which is its principal source of power. As Marx saw in the exploitation of the workers the source for capitalist profits, they see in the exploitation of the Third World the reason for the abundance in Western societies. But such a point of view is very simplistic, and limited to very few citizens of the technodemocracies. Most citizens still support with serenity the exploitation of their fellow citizens and even more easily support the exploitation of foreign workers who are far away and who belong to races that they consider inferior.

Rebellion does, however, undermine the Western system in a more direct way. Before the 1960s, the system seemed conclusively established. Europe was slipping little by little into American conformism. Socialist parties were gradually abandoning reformism as they had abandoned revolution. They were becoming a second management party facing the liberal-conservative coalition. The difference between the two was becoming just as small as that between the Republicans and the Democrats in the United States. Even the Communist parties of France and Italy seemed to be integrated into the system. Nobody could imagine that capitalism could be overthrown in the foreseeable future: rightists and leftists alike looked to the growth of production and the improvements in income that would make injustices less obvious. The rebelling students and the other marginal groups upset the tranquillity of these new Babbitts. Their socialism may be utopian and primitive, but they have revived the hope of socialism. Their vision of the economy is superficial and simplistic, but they have served notice that the increase in goods does not necessarily improve the quality of life, which is far more important than the gadgets popularized by advertising. They have touched upon the everyday absurdity of the industrial societies, their grayness, their emptiness, and their oppressiveness. These outsiders have made the citizens of the Western world understand that the king is indeed naked—something that in a confused fashion they felt but did not dare to admit. They will not forget it again. Now there is doubt about the future of their system.

The Basic Contradiction

The Western system now has the means to meet all the needs, both primary (food, shelter, clothing, security) and secondary (comfort, culture, recreation), of every person that lives in it. The economic oligarchy resists this development in order to keep in reserve a cheap work force that it can manipulate to hold down the demands of labor as a whole. The division of the workers into many unequal categories and the growth of corporate power enables it to maintain such a situation. But it cannot last forever. The technical capacity to initiate a society of abundance combines with the popular desire for such a society to engender a drive too strong to be contained for very long.

By doing away with the law of scarcity that had governed mankind from its very beginnings, technodemocracy made possible a fundamental upheaval in social relationships. The scarcity of available goods leads to bitter competition between men, no one of whom can be satisfied except at the expense of others. Abundance, on the other hand, makes it possible to realize, at least in part, the old dream of distributive justice: "to each according to his needs." Unquestionably, the structure of the Western nations and, in particular, the private ownership of the means of production prevent the establishment of strict equality: they tend to preserve the privileges of power and wealth enjoyed by the economic oligarchy. But these become more tolerable to the rest of the citizenry when everyone has a bearable standard of living.

This economic success of the Western system is achieved in part at the expense of the Third World, whose raw materials are bought at low prices by the industrial nations. There is no questioning their imperialism. But this is not the ultimate stage of capitalism. Capitalism deals with the underdeveloped countries as it does with its own workers: it

189

attempts to pay them as little as possible. If the unions exact high wages from it, it pays them more because it can: the productive capacity of its machines enables it to absorb the rise in costs entailed. It will capitulate in the same way on the prices of raw materials if their producers force it to do so by similar pressures. In this connection, the combined action of the Arab countries in oil sales is probably opening a new phase. What is more, better "terms of exchange," like a rise in wages, can broaden the potential market. Henry Ford's theories on employer-worker relations can be adapted to the relations between the industrial nations and the Third World. The fact remains that the industrial partners impose their will on the others insofar as they alone determine production. But this domination, too, becomes more tolerable when it is accompanied by a rise in the standard of living.

The Western system's economic success seems even greater when it is compared with the contemporary difficulties of the Socialist systems. Marx believed that a conflict would develop within capitalism between the forces of production, which were expanding by reason of technical advances, and the legal-political structure, which was tending toward stagnation or repression. In his view, only socialism, freed from private ownership and capable of organizing production on a macroeconomic scale, would be able to avoid such a conflict. The evolution of technodemocracy over the past twenty-five years is a challenge to such an analysis. Capitalist enterprises have adapted to the developments in the means of production; they have accelerated rather than slowed them. The law of progressive pauperization can be supported now only through interpretations that alter its meaning.

The conflict between the growth in the forces of production and the legal-political structures is more real in the Soviet Union and the people's democracies, whose economic difficulties are in marked contrast to the success of the West. It has already been pointed out that the comparison is probably invalidated by the fact that the advanced Socialist nations are currently going through a crisis of adjustment analogous to capitalism's in the 1930s; perhaps they will come out of it equally successfully. The fact remains that socialism today seems to be more effective in making possible the economic "take-off" of underdeveloped countries than in assuring the growth of hyperindustrialized nations.

But the staggering material success of the Western system is beginning to be accompanied by an unmistakable human loss. The pleasure of life—happiness, St.-Just would have said—does not develop at the same pace as the totals of production. On the contrary, it seems to be declining inversely as they advance. Cities are becoming uninhabitable just when almost everyone is compelled to live in them; nature is polluted and destroyed just when people feel a growing need to enjoy it; all modes of travel are intolerable just when journeys are increasing in number and length; old age takes on the proportions of a curse just when the ratio of the old to the young is rising; the grip of bigness is tightening just when everyone is acquiring the material and cultural means to enhance his own individuality; and so on.

The contradiction between the increase in the quantity of goods produced and the deterioration in the quality of life tends to become the major phenomenon of Western societies. It threatens to drive them into a much graver crisis than the rebellion of the 1960s, of which it was probably one of the causes. The question is, in fact, one of an inherent contradiction in the very nature of technodemocracy that tends to be exacerbated in direct proportion to the system's growth. It is engendered by the capitalist structure of production based on the law of profit. This structure assures productivity, growth, and innovation more efficiently than any other, and at the same time, by the same process, it causes a debasement of the quality of life.

The Western system attempts to hide this contradiction behind the theory of the "consumer society." It is alleged that the degradation of the quality of life in the industrial nations stems from economic expansion: that there is a contradiction between the quantity and the quality of the goods produced with the latter going down as quantity goes up. All developed countries, it is argued, find themselves in the same predicament. If it appears more serious in the advanced capitalist nations, that is because they are more developed than the socialist ones. They too will be faced with the same difficulties when they reach the level of abundance. This theory is widely held and the various rebellious groups have, despite their anticapitalistic stance, contributed to its success by reviving various arguments that have been advanced throughout history to oppose technical progress: the idea, developed by Cato the Elder, that frugality leads to the good life; the idea of moderation in all things that developed among the ancient Greeks; Christian beliefs in the virtue of abstinence; and so on.

191

But this theory of the consumer society cannot be accepted. A society of abundance offers greater opportunities for a pleasant life than a society based on poverty. However oppressive, the hardships caused by large organizations, the development of urban centers, and the pollution and degradation of nature, they are far less serious than the sufferings that stem from downright poverty. There is no common link between them and famine, epidemics, long and stupefying work, illiteracy, and so on. The present degradation of the quality of life in the Western societies results not from their economic expansion but from the manner in which profit and the profit motive determine this expansion.

It is technically possible today to build cities in which it would be a pleasure to live; all that is needed is to give priority to collective and cultural amenities, to the appurtenances of relaxation and leisure, to the harmony and beauty of the whole. Indeed, the industrial societies have available more of the means for attaining these ends than do traditional societies. But the pursuit of such objectives is socially and economically impossible in a capitalist system, in which the prime motivation for building mass housing is the profits to be made from it. Of course, the public authorities can take measures for the protection of collective interests. But the economic oligarchy does not permit such measures to be carried forward. The rise in population and the growth of cities occasioned by the development of production now make possible profits so huge that it is virtually impossible to exercise any control over the construction of housing.

The protection of nature is becoming equally impossible. Current campaigns against pollution and site destruction are doomed to failure in spite of some spectacular successes, the best example of which is the rescue of the Grand Canyon of the Colorado. But these isolated victories are drowned in an ocean of day-to-day defeats. The destruction of natural areas, the debasement of the countryside, the pollution of water and air increase inexorably. Here and there, the state or the local government takes some steps, which usually consist of making the taxpayers meet the costs of protection or purification, instead of charging them to the companies that are responsible for the damage. The international farce in connection with Venice is a fine instance of this. The chief peril to the city is posed by large industrial firms whose operations are changing the water balance in the lagoon. No one raises the question of relocating them; at most it is proposed that the whole world contribute to the cost of some protective measures of doubtful efficacy that would allow the companies to increase their profits undisturbed.

President Nixon had the courage to state the truth bluntly in Detroit in 1971, when he said: "We are not going to allow the problem of environment . . . to serve the destruction of the industrial system that has made our country great." Decoded, this means that the environment will be sacrificed to corporate profits. In fact, every Western nation follows this policy, with this single difference: their rulers, in general, do not admit it so openly. In a certain way this is reminiscent of the behavior of the fabulous animal that was so stupid that it ate its own limbs without even knowing it. Contemporary developments in capitalism in the advanced nations are leading to the same kind of self-destruction.

This kind of thinking is founded first of all on a conflict between individual profit and the collective interest. Liberal theory declares that the former guarantees the best development of the latter. This is true only within a narrow domain, that of productive capacity, and even there only within the framework of small and medium-sized enterprises rather than huge modern firms. On the total scale, the conflict is staggering. Car manufacturers will earn maximum profits by continuing to make the current kinds of engines, which poison the atmosphere and impair everyone's health and pleasure in living—including the motorist's. Builders of housing have the same motivation for saturation construction in the best parts of urban and natural areas without regard to community amenities, site protection, or the damage that they will thus be inflicting on the population as a whole and on their own customers. The stockholders of the Péchiney Company have the same reason for expanding the production of bauxite in Provence while destroying the beautiful Alpilles range.

There are other aspects of the way in which the imperative of profit gives to work that is most lucrative for its promoters priority over what would be most useful for the consumer. Cultural and community amenities are expensive and, as a rule, can be run only at a loss. So they are sacrificed. The consumer's own idea of what is useful is itself distorted by direct and indirect propaganda, the volume of which depends on the resources of the companies involved. Thus, large, established, concentrated industries have a considerable advantage. This mechanism made a great contribution to the development of the automobile in the West, which represents a major wastage and an important factor in the degradation of collective life. In a general way, advertising helps to achieve the hypertrophy of the manufacture of clothing, household products, and gadgets far beyond their real economic usefulness—in other words, beyond consumers' actual needs.

The analysis must be taken further. An economic system based on the supreme imperative of profit sacrifices the long to the short term, the future to the immediate. Once the manufactured product has been sold, the maker has his profit; it is of no importance to him what happens then to the buyer or the community. As far as perishable and semiperishable goods are concerned, since they must be constantly re-placed, the customer must in theory be satisfied if he is to go back to the same source. But determinations of quality are often difficult, and depend more on conditioning through advertising than on experience. What is more, such appraisals are always made in a narrow sense, being limited to the object purchased without regard to its impact on social life. The motorist rejoicing in his new Renault or Ford is hardly cog-nizant of the fact that the increase in traffic makes the cities into hells and poisons his own existence.

In certain areas, the conflict between the short and the long term is even more glaring and more profound. Many people hope to have apart-ments in pleasant neighborhoods or houses in a beautiful country area. The reputation of a given urban or rural area creates an excellent mar-ket for the new buildings erected there. Hence the rush of builders for such sites and their tendency toward maximum construction, which destroys the original charm of the place. But this the customers will recognize only afterward, as they live there, when the builders have already made their fortunes. The destruction of the Côte d'Azur in France and of the Balearic Isles and the Spanish seacoast are illustra-tions of this inexorable process that the growth of urbanization is spreading thoughout the West.

Furthermore, capitalism sacrifices intangible interests to monetary and economic profit. Ten years of mining in Baux-en-Provence is cer-tainly useful to national aluminum production. But no one has com-pared these advantages with the damage caused by the destruction of nature, which is less easy to evaluate in spite of being equally real.

Similarly, no one attempts any balance between the advantages created by green areas in a city, the esthetics of its buildings, the harmony in its planning, and the extra expenses imposed on builders of housing in order to achieve them. What is the worth to mankind of the charm of Piazza Navona, the nobility of Notre-Dame de Paris, the balance of Siena or Florence, the splendor of the Marseilles shoreline, and all the monuments, the places, the landscapes that make up "beauty"? The Western system does not include this in its accounting.

Until now, these basic defects were tolerable because European capitalism was expanding within the urban context created by the earlier aristocratic civilizations and American capitalism was developing in a vast virgin area of which it could destroy only small scattered sectors. Natural and historic environments retained their predominance in everyday life. But now the almost universal industrialization and urbanization compel virtually the entire population to live in a structure entirely subjugated to the law of profit, the inhuman quality of which can now be evaluated. The destruction of cities and of nature is increasing at ever growing speed. In a few years, the West will be immured in huge concrete megalopolises, in which the boredom of the inhabitants will mount as high as the profits of the promoters.

The pollution of the mind and the degradation of thought are no less obvious than the pollution of the cities and the deterioration of the quality of life. They stem from the same overall causes. The press, the radio, and television are excellent instruments of culture and freedom of thought—now available to all and not just to a small minority, as in the past. But they must be used in the proper way. Here again the new techniques have the potential to become the instruments of a new humanism, but the emphasis upon profit in the use of these media brings about the opposite result. They serve as instruments of advertising to expand production and sales and to increase profit. By serving short-term interests rather than long-term goals, the profit motive leads to the deculturation that has been described.

Some qualifications need to be added to this very general evaluation. But they would not modify it in any basic way. There can be hardly any question of the success of the Western system in terms of economic expansion, or of the fact that it has raised those societies that have practiced it close to the threshold of an abundance from which the Socialist nations are still far removed. Its failure in other areas that have to do with the quality of life is hardly more open to question. It appears established, finally, that quantitative success and qualitative failure result from the same essential factor: the imperative of profit, the foundation of capitalism. Thus, the Western system contains a basic contradiction that tends naturally to grow sharper.

There is no evidence, however, to show that the aggravation of this contradiction will lead to the collapse of technodemocracy in the foreseeable future. In this connection, three factors must be kept in mind. First of all, the myth of growth is deeply rooted in Western societies, and consequently there is a danger that production figures will long be regarded as more important than environmental and qualitative benefits. Even in the richest nations, the proportion of the poor—that is, of people whose primary or secondary needs remain unsatisfied to a substantial degree—is still high. Such people are naturally less sensitive to the quality of life than to the inadequacy of their living conditions. Even for the rest, the relative abundance is still too recent, too limited, and too tenuous to allow qualitative considerations to be important. The development of artificial needs through the conditioning of advertisement is a second factor that tends to maintain the drive for quantity rather than quality.

And third, whatever the flaws of the Western system in terms of quality of life, today they seem fewer than the corresponding faults in any other known system. If, in principle, socialism is superior to capitalism in this respect, since its basic motivation is the collective interest rather than individual profit, its practice is still far indeed from its theory. The Communist nations give more attention than do the technodemocracies to collective amenities, cultural development, community spirit, environmental protection. But at times their superiority gives the impression that it is the result of a lesser quantitative development—for instance, in the matter of automobile traffic or the deterioration of the cities through accelerated growth. Above all, their suppression of freedoms eliminates an essential aspect of the quality of life. As long as the governments of the Soviet Union, China, and the people's democracies continue to be the only practical examples and there is no development of a theory of socialism adapted to advanced liberal societies, capitalism will retain its strong position in the advanced nations that practice it.

Nor, finally, can one exclude the possibility that the Western system may adapt itself to the new situation that it must face. The flexibility and the innovative capacity that it has already demonstrated make this plausible. But such an adaptation is difficult in the present case, for the current conflict derives from the very foundation of the system—the profit imperative. No doubt, Janus' other face, political power, can help to restore the balance. In technodemocracies, the influence of the citizens can increase through political parties, trade unions, and mass organizations. If recognition of the qualitative debasement of life increases, popular pressure can counter industrial pressure to a certain degree.

But this presupposes a profound change in the relation of forces between the economic oligarchy and democratic power. The powerful means of pressure available to the oligarchy may lead to a different solution: a stabilization of technodemocracy not as a result of adjustment to the requirements of quality of life but through the adaptation of those requirement to its own structure. Conditioning through the press, television, and the other means of information and domination controlled by the oligarchy can in the end accustom people to the new collective environment that the Western system imposes on them. In 1966, this was regarded as the most likely outcome, on the theory that the West was slipping into a civilization of comfortable mediocrity, a kind of air-conditioned Byzantine Empire.

By opening people's eyes to such a future, by making them cognizant of the deterioration of their daily life, by showing them that the emperor was naked, by reviving doubts about technodemocracy, the rebels of the ensuing years slowed this trend. They did not halt it. Both faces of Janus would have to be brought into a better balance in order to cause any change in course, and this presupposes a growth of democracy in the face of an economic oligarchy whose technical progress heightens its power. In the end, a number of types of superstructure, all quite different, may evolve in the technodemocracies. The advent of one or another depends not on simple mechanical sequences but on a combination of complex factors in which the weight of traditional institutions, cultures, and behavior patterns is merged with that of current drives toward innovation and with special circumstances that may be present at any given moment in a given political system.

The notion of a convergence of systems is valid from an overall point of view. But one cannot predict the ryhthm and the timing. The West needs more socialism and the Socialist developed countries need more liberty. Scientific and technical development in the East will be impeded if individual initiative and freedom do not develop in all areas of life. But the impact of freedom will be limited in the West if collective interests and goals do not become the primary ends and replace private profit. But the two systems both have a great degree of flexibility and maneuverability, and these will allow for a long time to come the continuation of the neo-Stalinist pattern of the East and the neoliberal system in the West.